Use of Continuous Monitors and Autosamplers to Predict Unmeasured Water-Quality Constituents in Tributaries of the Tualatin River, Oregon

By Chauncey W. Anderson and Stewart A. Rounds

Prepared in cooperation with Clean Water Services

Scientific Investigations Report 2010–5008

U.S. Department of the Interior
U.S. Geological Survey

U.S. Department of the Interior
KEN SALAZAR, Secretary

U.S. Geological Survey
Marcia K. McNutt, Director

U.S. Geological Survey, Reston, Virginia: 2010

For more information on the USGS—the Federal source for science about the Earth, its natural and living resources, natural hazards, and the environment, visit http://www.usgs.gov or call 1-888-ASK-USGS

For an overview of USGS information products, including maps, imagery, and publications, visit http://www.usgs.gov/pubprod

To order this and other USGS information products, visit http://store.usgs.gov

Suggested citation:
Anderson, C.W., and Rounds, S.A., 2010, Use of continuous monitors and autosamplers to predict unmeasured water-quality constituents in tributaries of the Tualatin River, Oregon: U.S. Geological Survey Scientific Investigations Report 2010–5008, 76 p.

Contents

Figures

Figures—Continued

Tables

Tables—Continued

Conversion Factors and Datums

Conversion Factors

Inch/Pound to SI

Multiply	By	To obtain
cubic foot per second (ft³/s)	0.02832	cubic meter per second (m³/s)
foot (ft)	0.3048	meter (m)
inch (in.)	2.54	centimeter (cm)
mile (mi)	1.609	kilometer (km)
square mile (mi²)	2.590	square kilometer (km²)

SI to Inch/Pound

Multiply	By	To obtain
liter (L)	0.2642	gallon (gal)
milliliter (mL)	0.033814	ounce, fluid (fl. oz)
millimeter (mm)	0.03937	inch (in.)

Temperature in degrees Celsius (°C) may be converted to degrees Fahrenheit (°F) as follows:

$$°F = (1.8 \times °C) + 32.$$

Specific conductance is given in microsiemens per centimeter at 25 degrees Celsius (µS/cm at 25 °C).

Concentrations of chemical constituents in water are given either in milligrams per liter (mg/L) or micrograms per liter (µg/L).

Datums

Horizontal coordinate information is referenced to either the North American Datum of 1927 (NAD 27) or 1983 (NAD 83) as noted in the text.

Abbreviations and Acronyms

BCF	bias corrections factor
Ci	concentration from a depth- and width-integrated sample
Cp	concentration from a pumped sampler
Cs	ambient stream concentration at the point of intake
CWS	Clean Water Services
E. coli	*Escherichia coli*
FNU	formazin nephelometric units
NWIS	National Water Information System
OWRD	Oregon Water Resources Department
ORWSC	U. S. Geological Survey Oregon Water Science Center
R^2	coefficient of determination
RMSE	root mean square error
SRS	standard reference samples
SSC	suspended sediment concentration
TMDL	Total Maximum Daily Load
TKN	total Kjeldahl nitrogen
TP	total phosphorus
TSS	total suspended solids
USGS	U.S. Geological Survey
VIF	variance inflation factor
VIF_{crit}	critical level for VIF calculated from the model's adjusted-R^2

Use of Continuous Monitors and Autosamplers to Predict Unmeasured Water-Quality Constituents in Tributaries of the Tualatin River, Oregon

By Chauncey W. Anderson and Stewart A. Rounds

Abstract

Management of water quality in streams of the United States is becoming increasingly complex as regulators seek to control aquatic pollution and ecological problems through Total Maximum Daily Load programs that target reductions in the concentrations of certain constituents. Sediment, nutrients, and bacteria, for example, are constituents that regulators target for reduction nationally and in the Tualatin River basin, Oregon. These constituents require laboratory analysis of discrete samples for definitive determinations of concentrations in streams. Recent technological advances in the nearly continuous, in situ monitoring of related water-quality parameters has fostered the use of these parameters as surrogates for the labor intensive, laboratory-analyzed constituents. Although these correlative techniques have been successful in large rivers, it was unclear whether they could be applied successfully in tributaries of the Tualatin River, primarily because these streams tend to be small, have rapid hydrologic response to rainfall and high streamflow variability, and may contain unique sources of sediment, nutrients, and bacteria.

This report evaluates the feasibility of developing correlative regression models for predicting dependent variables (concentrations of total suspended solids, total phosphorus, and *Escherichia coli* bacteria) in two Tualatin River basin streams: one draining highly urbanized land (Fanno Creek near Durham, Oregon) and one draining rural agricultural land (Dairy Creek at Highway 8 near Hillsboro, Oregon), during 2002–04. An important difference between these two streams is their response to storm runoff; Fanno Creek has a relatively rapid response due to extensive upstream impervious areas and Dairy Creek has a relatively slow response because of the large amount of undeveloped upstream land. Four other stream sites also were evaluated, but in less detail. Potential explanatory variables included continuously monitored streamflow (discharge), stream stage, specific conductance, turbidity, and time (to account for seasonal processes). Preliminary multiple-regression models were identified using stepwise regression and Mallow's Cp, which maximizes regression correlation coefficients and accounts for the loss of additional degrees of freedom when extra explanatory variables are used. Several data scenarios were created and evaluated for each site to assess the representativeness of existing monitoring data and autosampler-derived data, and to assess the utility of the available data to develop robust predictive models. The goodness-of-fit of candidate predictive models was assessed with diagnostic statistics from validation exercises that compared predictions against a subset of the available data.

The regression modeling met with mixed success. Functional model forms that have a high likelihood of success were identified for most (but not all) dependent variables at each site, but there were limitations in the available datasets, notably the lack of samples from high-flows. These limitations increase the uncertainty in the predictions of the models and suggest that the models are not yet ready for use in assessing these streams, particularly under high-flow conditions, without additional data collection and recalibration of model coefficients. Nonetheless, the results reveal opportunities to use existing resources more efficiently. Baseline conditions are well represented in the available data, and, for the most part, the models reproduced these conditions well. Future sampling might therefore focus on high flow conditions, without much loss of ability to characterize the baseline. Seasonal cycles, as represented by trigonometric functions of time, were not significant in the evaluated models, perhaps because the baseline conditions are well characterized in the datasets or because the other explanatory variables indirectly incorporate seasonal aspects. Multicollinearity among independent variables was minimal and had little effect on model selection or the value of model coefficients.

Automated unattended samplers were used to supplement the monitoring data used in this study, and a detailed quality assurance program was used to assess the accuracy and representativeness of samples collected using autosamplers. Care must be taken to avoid serial correlation among samples when autosamplers are used to collect multiple samples within individual storms. However, the results showed that autosamplers can provide high-quality data from small streams during storm-runoff conditions, thereby offering a cost-effective and convenient means of augmenting manually collected samples and collecting samples at high flows that otherwise might be missed by existing monitoring programs.

Introduction

Since the early 1990s, the quality of water and ecological health of tributaries to the Tualatin River in northwestern Oregon (fig. 1) have been the subject of heightened concern from resource managers, regulators, and citizen groups. The small urban and agricultural streams on the eastern side of the basin are known to have water-quality problems, but the magnitude, duration, seasonality, and short- and long-term trends for those concerns have not been well characterized. Aspects of those problems have been studied, including low-flow phosphorus and bacteria levels (McCarthy, 2000),

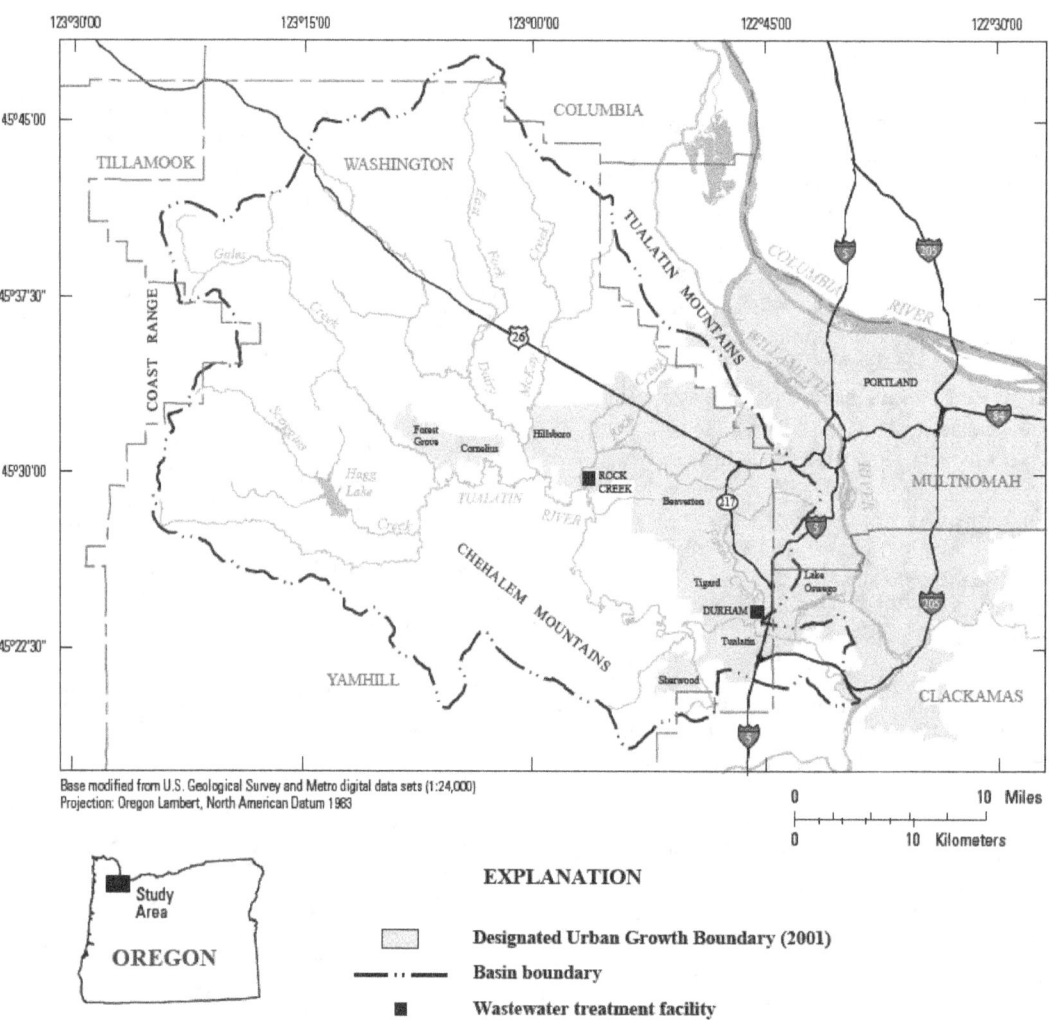

Figure 1.   Tualatin River basin, Oregon.

storm-related variations in nutrient and bacteria concentrations (Anderson and Rounds, 2003), and the levels of trace metals and organochlorine pesticides in fish tissue and sediment (Bonn, 1999). Issues of high water temperature, excessive bacteria levels, high phosphorus concentrations, and low dissolved oxygen concentrations were cited as particular problems requiring attention in Tualatin River tributaries in the 2001 revision of the Total Maximum Daily Load (TMDL) regulations for the basin (Oregon Department of Environmental Quality, 2001). Increased monitoring and additional studies have helped to fill gaps in our understanding of the dynamics of water quality in these streams. The characterization of the short-term dynamics, long-term trends, and spatial variations of water quality in these systems, however, probably will require the use of new approaches.

The use of submersible instruments that simultaneously measure and log multiple water-quality parameters in situ is growing rapidly in the Pacific Northwest and nationally. Such instruments can collect data at regular intervals and for long periods without human intervention, thereby providing opportunities for increased data collection at reduced costs. These instruments often are referred to as continuous monitors because they can be operated continuously for long periods. Data from continuous monitors can be used for many purposes, including (1) documentation of routine or event-based environmental conditions in a drainage basin, (2) detection of daily and seasonal variations and long-term trends in water quality, (3) calibration and validation of numerical models, (4) feedback for regulatory and resource management systems, and (5) surrogate measurements for the calculation of concentrations or loads of suspended sediment (Gray and Glysson, 2003; Uhrich and Bragg, 2003) or other constituents (Christensen and others, 2000). Monitored parameters typically include water temperature, specific conductance, pH, and, increasingly, dissolved oxygen, turbidity, and chlorophyll. Many other types of sensors are under development.

Despite the advantages of these continuous monitors, many constituents of interest to regulators and resource managers still cannot be directly measured by such technology. For example, streams in the Pacific Northwest often are managed for their concentrations of suspended sediment (or total suspended solids), various nutrients (nitrogen and phosphorus species), or bacterial pathogens (such as *Escherichia coli* [*E. coli*] as an indicator of bacterial pathogens). No routine and direct in situ measurements can be done for these constituents at environmentally relevant concentrations by currently available commercial instruments. Such analyses, therefore, must be made in a laboratory using discreet samples collected from the stream.

Data from continuous monitors, however, sometimes can provide an indication of the concentrations of unmeasured constituents. For example, turbidity in water often is directly dependent on suspended sediment concentration (Lewis, 1996;

Anderson and Rounds, 2003; Gray and Glysson, 2003; Uhrich and Bragg, 2003); therefore, turbidity data from continuous monitors can be used to estimate a time series of suspended sediment concentration. Christensen and others (2000) used data from continuous monitors in Kansas streams to calculate instantaneous concentrations and loads of alkalinity, dissolved solids, total suspended solids (TSS), chloride, sulfate, atrazine, and fecal coliform bacteria. Site-specific regressions between monitored parameters and the results of discrete water samples were derived for these constituents, and the regressions were then applied to long-term monitor records at the study sites to estimate a time series of constituent concentrations. By combining these concentration estimates with discharge information, constituent loads also can be estimated. For example, Uhrich and Bragg (2003), Anderson (2007), and Bragg and others (2007) performed similar calculations using continuous records of turbidity and discharge to estimate suspended sediment concentrations and loads in the North Santiam and McKenzie Rivers, respectively, in western Oregon.

To use continuous monitors to develop robust statistical models for sampled water-quality constituents, independent samples representing a broad range of conditions (high- and low-flow and seasonal warm/cold or spring/summer/autumn/winter) are needed at each site. Clean Water Services, the primary wastewater and stormwater management utility in the urban areas of Washington County, Oregon, has been collecting routine water-quality samples at many sites in the Tualatin River basin for more than 20 years. Most samples collected, however, represented low- or base-flow conditions, and were not targeted for storms. The U.S. Geological Survey (USGS) has collected data for many years and for various purposes at Fanno Creek near Durham, including during a few storms, but these data also are of limited scope. Data from these two sources were used to evaluate the potential regression models for this study.

Like continuous monitors, automatic samplers (referred to as autosamplers in this report) can collect water samples at night, during storms, or at specific intervals without the need for human operators. An autosampler can collect multiple samples (typically as many as 24) before it must be restocked with empty bottles. The autosampler also can be refrigerated or stocked with ice to minimize sample degradation. After collection, samples from the autosamplers (or autosamples) are retrieved and analyzed at a laboratory for the water-quality constituents of interest. Autosamplers can be programmed to collect samples at prescribed intervals of time or flow, and can be triggered by specific conditions. Used together, a continuous monitor can trigger an autosampler during an event (for example, when conditions exceed some threshold measured by the monitor) and can thereby document water-quality conditions in the stream at the time of sample collection.

Continuous monitors and autosamplers offer many advantages over manual sampling, including the potential to collect many samples and large amounts of data during a short time, when the number of sites is large, if the sites are remote, or if the sites are difficult or inconvenient to access (such as at night, on weekends, or under hazardous conditions). These advantages are particularly useful when trying to characterize short-term variations in stream conditions during storms at multiple sites. Collecting an adequate number of samples at multiple sites during a storm with a crew of technicians can be inefficient and expensive compared to the use of remote and automated instruments, if they can accomplish the same tasks.

Despite these advantages, continuous monitors and autosamplers are subject to mechanical malfunction, sampling bias, or both, and require a certain degree of quality control to assure that the resulting data are accurate and representative of stream conditions. The quality control issues include the degree to which measurements or samples collected at one location in the stream by the autosampler represent conditions throughout the stream cross section, measurement bias because of fouling or sensor drift of deployed monitors, the possibility of carryover contamination because autosampler tubing was not completely cleaned, and the potential for exceeding prescribed sample holding times or temperatures in autosamplers. These issues must be addressed to ensure proper use of this technology.

This report uses correlative techniques that have been shown to work with relative success in various geologic regions (Christensen and others, 2000; Lietz and Debiak, 2005; Rasmussen and others, 2008), although the rivers studied typically have been larger than the Tualatin River tributaries. Application of these techniques was attempted in small Pacific Northwest streams that have large changes in characteristics between low and high flow, and in agricultural and urban areas. As part of a long-term scientific collaboration between the USGS and Clean Water Services, this study evaluated the quantity and attributes of data that are necessary to build useful predictive models for such streams.

Purpose and Scope

The purpose of this report is to evaluate the use of continuous monitors and autosamplers to collect representative and accurate water samples over a range of stream conditions,

and to construct and demonstrate the use of preliminary predictive statistical models of unmeasured water-quality constituents in selected tributaries to the Tualatin River. Specifically, the objectives were to

1. Evaluate the use of autosamplers for unattended sampling in conjunction with continuous monitors and evaluate the quality of autosamples;

2. Develop preliminary regression models to predict the concentrations of selected water-quality constituents using concurrent data from continuous monitors, and evaluate the robustness and accuracy of those models;

3. Evaluate the adequacy of available laboratory data to augment autosampler-derived data for developing regression models that estimate constituent concentrations and loads;

4. Use the regression models to predict and evaluate time series concentrations and to develop uncertainty estimates for modeled constituent concentrations from historical continuous monitor data at the same sites; and

5. Identify potential changes to sampling strategies that would allow future monitoring efforts to improve the regression models developed.

Sites on six selected tributaries in the Tualatin River basin were studied from June 2002 through December 2003. The sites represented a range of upstream land uses, from intense urban development to rural agricultural and forested areas. Continuous, in situ monitors recorded stage, streamflow, water temperature, specific conductance, dissolved oxygen, pH, and turbidity. Autosamples were analyzed for a suite of nutrients (nitrogen and phosphorus species), total suspended solids, chloride, and bacteria (*E. coli*) over a range of stream conditions. Approximately 48 discrete autosamples were collected at each site over the course of two or three storm events. The model-building process was augmented by additional data from USGS and Clean Water Services databases, covering the study period 2002–07.

Full development of example models was limited to two target sites—Fanno Creek near Durham Road, and Dairy Creek at Highway 8 near Hillsboro. Data from USGS and Clean Water Services databases were used to augment the autosampler data. The additional USGS and Clean Water

Services data were concurrent with the dates of monitor deployment and, together with the continuous monitor data, were used to evaluate calibration and validation scenarios for these sites. For the remaining four non-target sites, preliminary model forms were identified but no additional data exploration was performed. Data were compiled for all samples collected using continuous monitors and autosamplers, but model development was limited to three whole-water constituents of primary interest to Clean Water Services and other local regulatory and resource-management agencies, specifically total suspended solids (TSS), total phosphorus (TP), and *E. coli* bacteria.

Study Area Description

The Tualatin River is a major tributary to the Willamette River near Portland in northwestern Oregon (fig. 1). The characteristics of the Tualatin River basin have been described in several reports, including those by Kelly and others (1999) and Rounds and Wood (2001). The basin has undergone rapid urbanization since the late 1980s and is now home to about half a million people, mainly in the central and eastern part of the basin and within the urban growth boundary of the Portland metropolitan area. Beyond the urban growth boundary, the fertile soil of the valley floor supports a wide variety of agricultural activities. The Coast Range Mountains to the west are densely forested and are a source for water supply and lumber production.

In an attempt to improve water quality in the Tualatin River and address specific issues related to algal growth and periodic high pH and low dissolved oxygen conditions, TMDLs for ammonia and phosphorus were set for the Tualatin River and its major tributaries in 1988 (Oregon Department of Environmental Quality, 1997), but primarily focused on the main stem Tualatin River. After the establishment of the TMDLs, studies of water quality in the main stem of the Tualatin River have highlighted the role of its tributaries as sources of TMDL constituents and oxygen-depleting substances to the main stem (Kelly, 1997). Results from the previous studies indicated that more information is needed on these constituents in the tributaries, and updated methods are needed to document their concentrations and delivery to the main stem during storm runoff periods.

When the Tualatin River TMDLs were revised in 2001, the tributaries received greater attention. New TMDLs for water temperature, bacteria, and oxygen-depleting substances were created, and modified limits on ammonia and phosphorus were retained (Oregon Department of Environmental Quality, 2001). Although the tributaries certainly affect the quality of water in the Tualatin River to some degree, the 2001 TMDLs demonstrated that the water quality and ecological health of the tributaries also was important.

Some river and tributary issues, such as high water temperature, algal growth, high pH, and low dissolved oxygen occur mainly during summer and autumn low-flow conditions, although high bacteria levels tend to be most problematic during storm events. An adequate characterization of the water-quality and ecological issues in the tributaries must include a good understanding of system behavior under a wide variety of conditions and time scales, and should address issues related to nutrients, bacteria, suspended solids, and other TMDL-related parameters. This study was designed to use continuous monitors to estimate some of these quantities, such as TP, TSS, and *E. coli* bacteria, and thereby aid in developing a better understanding of the dynamics of these parameters and how they affect stream quality.

Sites representing the broad range of land uses and hydrology in the basin were selected for development of regression models. The largest tributaries of the Tualatin River include Gales Creek (mainly forested), Dairy Creek (largely agricultural), Rock Creek (mixed urban), and Fanno Creek (urban). These creeks account for a large fraction of the drainage in the Tualatin River basin. A site on Beaverton Creek, a tributary to Rock Creek, has a large amount of upstream commercial and urban land use. Chicken Creek, a small tributary to the Tualatin River, was included because it drains a rapidly expanding urban and rural-residential area in the southern part of the basin. The locations and characteristics of these sites are shown in figure 2 and table 1. These creeks have water-quality problems that would benefit from further characterization.

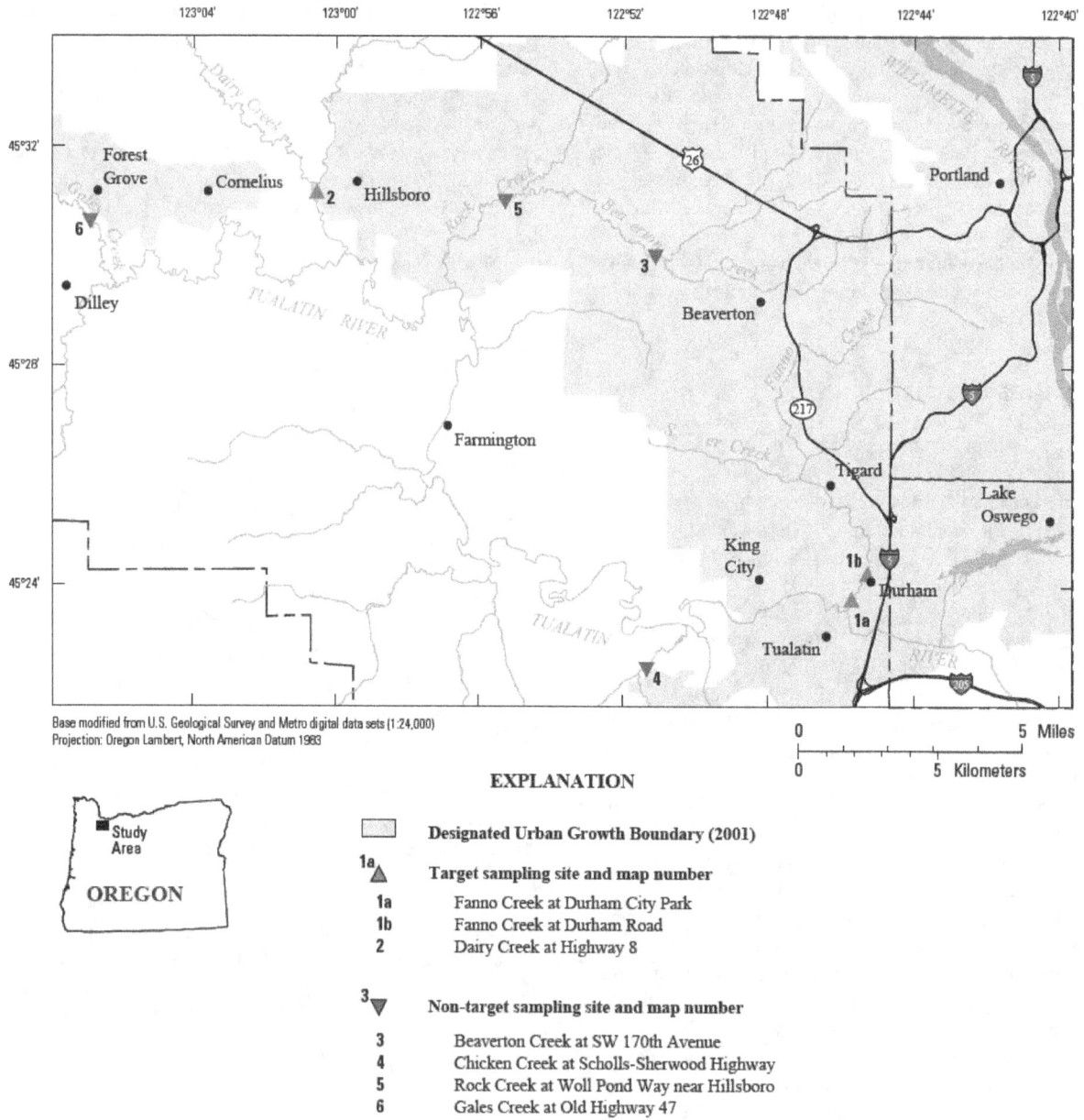

Figure 2. Locations of sites selected for development of regression models for unmeasured water-quality constituents in the Tualatin River basin, Oregon, 2002–04.

Table 1. Sampling sites and characteristics in tributaries of the Tualatin River basin, Oregon, 2002–04.

[Target sites are those where data analysis included data from autosampler deployment plus historical data from U S Geological Survey and Clean Water Services databases, and model development included more extensive calibration and validation processes Non-target sites were sites included in this study but where data analysis was limited to preliminary identification of model forms based on analysis of autosampler data alone The site at Fanno Creek was moved from Durham City Park to Durham Road in 2003 **Latitude and Longitude**, in degrees, minutes, seconds, are based on North American Datum of 1927 (NAD 27) **Streamflow data source:** Stream-flow data were obtained from U S Geological Survey (USGS) or Oregon Water Resources Department (OWRD) gaging stations Data from on-site gaging stations were used directly; data from upstream gaging stations were routed and travel times estimated as described in text Drainage areas are from StreamStats (http://water usgs gov/osw/streamstats/index html) **Abbreviations:** mi, mile; mi^2, square mile]

Station name	Map No.	Station identification No.	Latitude	Longitude	Streamflow data source	Drainage area (mi^2)	Primary upstream land use	Monitor deployment dates
				Target sites				
Fanno Creek at Durham City Park	1a	452348122454701	45°23'49"	122°45'43"	USGS (0 25 mi upstream)	31 7	Urban	Spring–autumn, 2001–02
Fanno Creek at Durham Road	1b	14206950	45°24'13"	122°45'13"	USGS	31 5	Urban	Continuous, September 2002–current
Dairy Creek at Highway 8	2	453113123003501	45°31'13"	123°00'35"	OWRD	229	Agricultural	Spring-autumn, 2001–03; Continuous, 2004–current
				Non-target sites				
Beaverton Creek at SW 170th Avenue	3	453004122510301	45°30'04"	122°51'03"	Routed from upstream OWRD gaging stations	22 8	Urban	Spring–autumn, 2001–03; Continuous, 2004–current
Chicken Creek at Scholls-Sherwood Highway	4	452230122512201	45°22'30"	122°51'22"	OWRD	15 3	Urban and agricultural	Spring–autumn, 2001–current
Rock Creek at Woll Pond Way near Hillsboro	5	453104122551201	45°31'04"	122°55'12"	Routed from upstream OWRD gaging stations	65	Urban	Spring–autumn, 2001–03
Gales Creek at Old Highway 47	6	453040123065201	45°30'40"	123°06'52"	OWRD	74 7	Forested	Spring–autumn, 2001–06; Continuous, 2007–current

Methods

Data Sources

Data used for the regression models were obtained from four primary sources. Continuous streamflow data were obtained from stream-gaging stations (table 1) operated by USGS or the Oregon Water Resources Department (OWRD). Continuous data for field parameters (specific conductance and turbidity) were obtained from monitors operated by USGS at each site (table 1) for the study period or longer, although the monitors were removed at some sites during high flow in winter. Water-quality data for sampled constituents such as TSS, nutrients, and *E. coli* bacteria were obtained from autosamplers deployed during the study period (appendix A) and from historical datasets maintained by USGS (2001–07) and Clean Water Services (2001–04).

USGS data primarily were available for the Fanno Creek at Durham Road site and were collected for various purposes; most high-flow water-quality data available for the Fanno Creek site were from the USGS historical database. Analyses included nutrients, suspended sediment, trace and major elements, and dissolved pesticides; however, only suspended sediment and TP were used for this report. Microbiological sampling, including *E. coli* bacteria, generally was not done by USGS during this period. Clean Water Services collects water-quality samples at least monthly at each of the study sites, and sometimes weekly, as part of its ambient monitoring program; however, high-flow periods are not specifically targeted and typically are under-represented in the Clean Water Services database. Clean Water Services sample analyses routinely include TSS, nutrients, and *E. coli* bacteria, among others.

For the Dairy Creek site, Clean Water Services ambient monitoring data are the only available historical data, and are primarily from monthly samples. In addition, the available explanatory data are limited at this site because the continuous monitor was not deployed during winter until 2004–05. Finally, under certain conditions, streamflow at Dairy Creek can be affected by backwater from the Tualatin River, a situation that might invalidate any correlations established for unhindered flow conditions.

Monitors

Continuous water-quality monitors were operated according to standard USGS protocols (Wagner and others, 2006). All monitors were the same, a YSI Environmental model 6920 multiparameter sonde equipped with probes to measure water temperature, specific conductance, turbidity, pH, and dissolved oxygen. Turbidity probes were YSI model 6026 probes, with the data reported in Formazin Nephelometric Units, or FNU (Anderson, 2004). Deployed monitors were cleaned and calibrated regularly, typically at 2-week intervals, and corrections due to cleaning and calibration were recorded. Data from the monitors were loaded into the USGS database and corrected to account for the effects of biofouling and sensor calibration drift according to procedures outlined by Wagner and others (2006).

Each monitor was deployed in a 6-in. diameter PVC pipe mounted vertically on a steel post midstream at a height of approximately 6 in. to 1 ft above the streambed, with a locking cap for protection. The PVC pipe was perforated generously at the bottom to allow free circulation of stream water around the probes. Data were collected hourly. Periodically, and at a range of streamflows, the cross-sectional variation of monitor parameters was examined by making instantaneous measurements in a transect with a calibrated multiparameter instrument, and comparing the results to those logged by the monitor. The observed cross-sectional variability never exceeded the allowed calibration tolerances of the instruments; therefore, it was not necessary to adjust the monitor data to account for observed cross-sectional variations.

Values for field parameters used in the regressions (specific conductance and turbidity) were obtained from the USGS continuous monitors rather than the Clean Water Services database when possible, for two reasons. Primarily, for making predictions of water-quality constituents during unsampled periods, the monitor data (and stream gages) are the only available source of independent variables. Therefore, the data used for constructing regressions should be collected in the same manner and be as internally consistent as the data used for making predictions. Secondly, turbidity data are known to be highly dependent on the optical configuration of the probe and potentially even the instrument model used (Anderson, 2004); therefore, consistency in long-term data collection methods is a critical factor when using turbidity as a surrogate for other parameters. For these reasons, the USGS has used the same models of turbidity probes throughout the monitoring network in the Tualatin River basin since their installation. Clean Water Services field data are from similar instruments, but calibration techniques and data

management (especially policies on shifting data according to calibration errors) are different from those used by USGS. Furthermore, the Clean Water Services laboratory uses a bench top meter to measure turbidity, which is likely to produce different results than the USGS monitors because of critical methodological differences (Anderson, 2004). Nonetheless, for some periods, particularly at the Dairy Creek site where the USGS monitor was removed each winter during 2002–04, data from the continuous monitors were unavailable and Clean Water Services data were occasionally used to calibrate the regression models.

For purposes unrelated to this study, the monitoring site in Fanno Creek was moved in 2003 from Durham City Park (fig. 2, site 1a) about 0.25 mi upstream to Durham Road (fig. 2; site 1b). Monitor and autosampler data were from the Durham City Park site until January 10, 2003, and from the Durham Road site thereafter. The potential influence of moving this station on development and interpretation of the regression models is discussed in the "Relations Between Continuous Monitor Data and Selected Water-Quality Constituents" section.

Streamflow was continuously recorded at some sites (see table 1), either by USGS (Rantz and others, 1982) or by OWRD, according to standard USGS methods. The Dairy Creek site at Highway 8, which is about 2 mi from its junction with the Tualatin River, is susceptible to backwater from the Tualatin River during high flows in winter. Oregon Water Resources Department (ORWD) considers the stage-discharge rating at this site to be unreliable at a stage greater than about 10 ft (D. Hedin, Oregon Water Resources Department, written commun., July 2008), although the rating may be reliable at stages as high as 15–16 ft when flows in the Tualatin River are not high. OWRD does not provide streamflow records for stages greater than 10 ft at this site. At the non-target sites Rock Creek and Beaverton Creek, which were ungaged, streamflow records at the monitor site were reconstructed by simple summation and routing of upstream, recorded discharges. Travel times from upstream sites were estimated by examining streamflow data at upstream sites combined with monitor data (especially turbidity and specific conductance) during storms to determine the timing of discharge peaks. The difference in timing of the peaks was used to linearly adjust upstream discharges to represent flow at the downstream sites. Attempting to simulate the discharge record during storms at the Beaverton and Rock Creek sites in this manner (that is, without a more extensive hydrologic modeling approach) exposed difficulties in the use of discharge as an independent variable for developing predictive regression models at ungaged sites, contributing to these sites' consideration as non-target rather than target sites.

Autosamplers

Autosamplers were operated as temporary installations for the duration of each storm or sampling event. Autosamplers used were ISCO, Inc., Model 6712 portable samplers, equipped with level sensors. Samplers were placed in a secure, level position on the streambank adjacent to the continuous monitors. Where possible, the samplers were housed in portable, locking fiberglass enclosures. Each sampler included a peristaltic pump to draw water from the stream through 3/8-in. inner-diameter vinyl tubing. Together with a communications cable from the water-quality monitor, this tubing was anchored to concrete blocks along the streambed. The intake tubing was positioned following USGS guidelines as summarized by G.D. Glysson, U.S. Geological Survey, written commun., 2009, and shown in table 2, except for items 3–5, which could not be determined with available resources for the study sites. The mouth of the vinyl tubing was secured to the perforated section of the monitor casing, oriented along the direction of flow and pointing downstream, an orientation that has been shown to minimize adverse sampling effects for pumping samplers (Winterstein, 1986). Because of pumping constraints, efforts were made to minimize the length of tubing between the monitor and the autosampler, typically 12 to 25 ft, with resultant vertical heads between 2 and 10 ft. Complete elimination of dips in the tubing that might trap heavy sediment particles was not possible; however, an effort was made to minimize the dips in the tubing.

Each autosampler was configured with a carousel holding twenty-four 1-L polyethylene bottles. Prior to each deployment, the vinyl tubing and polyethylene bottles were cleaned with hot tap water and phosphorus-free detergent and thoroughly rinsed with deionized water. Upon deployment, the middle of the carousel in the autosampler was loaded with ice. Once deployed, samplers were visited at least once daily to check on the operation of the monitor and the sampler, and to change sample bottles, batteries, or ice, as necessary.

Table 2. U.S. Geological Survey guidelines for placement of autosampler intake.

[From G D Glysson, U S Geological Survey, written commun , 2009 **Abbreviations:** mm, millimeter]

1. Select a stable cross section of reasonably uniform depth and width to maximize the stability of the relation between concentration at a point and the mean concentration in the cross section. This guideline is of primary importance in the decision to use an automatic sampler in a given situation; if a reasonably stable relation between the sample-point concentration and mean cross-section concentration cannot be attained by the following outlined steps, the sampler should not be installed and an alternate location should be considered. If banks are unstable and the sampler has to be installed in that location, install the intake on the cutting side of the channel so that the intake will not be buried.

2. Consider only the part of the vertical that could be sampled using a standard U.S Geological Survey depth- or point-integrating sampler, excluding the unsampled zone, because data collected with a depth- or point-integrating sampler will be used to calibrate the pumping sampler. (See Edwards and Glysson, 1999, fig. 1.)

3. Determine, if possible, the depth of the point of mean concentration in each vertical for each size class of particles finer than 0.250 mm, from a series of carefully collected point-integrated samples.

4. Determine, if possible, the mean depth of occurrence of the mean concentration in each vertical for all particles finer than 0.250 mm.

5. Use the mean depth of occurrence of the mean concentration in the cross section as a reference depth for placement of the intake.

6. Adjust the depth location of the intake to avoid interference by dune migration or contamination by bed material.

7. Adjust the depth location of the intake to ensure submergence at all times.

8. Locate the intake laterally in the streamflow at a distance far enough from the bank to eliminate any possible bank effects.

9. Place the intake in a zone of high velocity and turbulence to improve distribution by mixing, reduce possible deposition on or near the intake, and provide for rapid removal of any particles disturbed during the purge cycle. Avoid placing the intake in an eddy, as it will probably not be representative of the water in the cross section.

10. Consideration must be given to placing the intake and tubing in a place so that they will be protected during high streamflows.

The water-quality monitor and a separate water-level sensor were interfaced with the autosampler's programmable computer. The ISCO water-level sensor used a pressure gage to sense the back pressure on air bubbled slowly through a small diameter tubing, the mouth of which was anchored to a fixed position in the stream. The water-level sensors proved to be unreliable and ultimately were used only for qualitative purposes to verify the timing of the streamflow peak rather than as a trigger for sampling or for depth data that could be used for correlations. Therefore, the autosamplers were programmed to use only turbidity data from the continuous monitor and were interrogated at 5-minute intervals, to trigger the sampling. Turbidity was considered the most reliable indicator that the stream was responding to a storm; an increase in turbidity of 10–15 FNU typically was used as the threshold for beginning sampling. Once triggered, the samplers were programmed to collect samples hourly, with a maximum of 24 bottles, and to record the monitor data and the time when each sample was collected. Prior to collecting each sample, the autosampler purged the vinyl sample tubing with air to remove any residual water and sediment, then performed three complete stream-water rinses of the line between the stream-end of the tubing and the liquid detector at the peristaltic pump head. Upon successful sample collection, the numbered bottles were retrieved and transported on ice to the Clean Water Services water-quality laboratory. The position of each bottle in the carousel was recorded, and the sampling data (timing of sample collection, water level, and water-quality data from the continuous monitor) were downloaded from the autosampler. Autosampler data from this study are reported in appendix A.

Autosampler Quality Assurance

Several issues potentially affecting the quality of data from autosampler-collected samples were identified and investigated at the beginning of the study. These included possible cross-contamination of samples from the vinyl autosampler tubing, which could not be washed between individual samples, and the degree to which samples collected by the autosampler at a point in the stream were comparable to those collected by standard USGS depth- and width-integrating and ultra-clean sampling protocols (Horowitz and others, 1994; Edwards and Glysson, 1999; G.D. Glysson, U.S. Geological Survey, written commun., 2009) .

Cross-contamination initially was assessed in the laboratory by manually directing the sampler to collect a sequence of samples (three replicates each) from vats containing the following materials:

1. Clean distilled and deionized water,

2. Mixture of tap water and suspended soil,

3. Clean deionized water,

4. Deionized water with a high-nutrient synthetic standard, prepared by the USGS Oregon Water Science Center (previously described by Anderson and Rounds [2003, appendix A]), and

5. Deionized water with a low-nutrient synthetic standard.

The resuspended mixture of tap water and soil (step 2 above) could not be uniformly mixed; therefore, results were not expected to be precise for analyses affected by particulates in water, such as TP. The point of using the soil mixture was to evaluate the extent of carryover of particulates to the subsequent deionized water samples. Samples from this series of tests were analyzed for nutrients (whole and filtered water) and chloride (filtered). For the synthetic standard samples, these tests also functioned as an evaluation of accuracy and precision in the sampling-analysis process.

The results of this series of tests generally were good and indicated that carryover of contamination from sample to sample using autosamplers with appropriately cleaned and maintained equipment was minimal, and could not be distinguished from background laboratory contamination levels (table 3). A low level of contamination of blank water by soluble reactive phosphorus was detected in laboratory blank samples shown in table 3 (test 1, 0.009 mg/L as P) and in two of three initial blank tests through the autosamplers (test 4, 0.007 mg/L as P). Only one sample indicated a small carryover of suspended material, as measured by total Kjeldahl nitrogen (TKN), a low concentration (test 6, 0.055 mg/L as N) just above the detection limit, in the first blank deionized water replicate following the soil mixtures. Considering that environmental concentrations of nutrients in storm runoff in the study streams were expected to be approximately 5–10 times higher than any contamination level detected in these tests, it was determined that neither contamination nor carryover was a major problem from the autosampler configuration.

Table 3. Results of laboratory quality-assurance tests of autosamplers.

[Results in **bold** indicate potential contamination or carryover. Results in *italics* represent statistics or values not derived from the laboratory. **Abbreviations:** DI, distilled, deionized water; SRS, Standard Reference Sample; <, less than; N/A, not applicable]

Test sequence	Sampling method	Purpose	Medium	Replicate No.	Total suspended solids (mg/L)	Ammonium-nitrogen (mg/L as N)	Total Kjeldahl nitrogen (mg/L as N)	Total phosphorus (mg/L as P)	Soluble reactive phosphorus (mg/L as P)	Chloride (mg/L)	Comments
1	Direct pour (no autosampler)	Test of lab cleanliness	DI	1	N/A	<0.01	<0.05	<0.025	**0.00**	<0.25	Tests 1–3 are analysis of source materials, for comparison with results of samples collected with the autosampler in tests 4,6,7,8.
				2	N/A	<0.01	<0.05	<0.025	<0.005	<0.25	
	Median					*<0.01*	*<0.05*	*<0.025*	*0.007*	*<0.25*	
2	Direct pour (no autosampler)	Test of lab accuracy	SRS, low	N/A	N/A	0.608	0.292	0.073	0.038	5.6	
	Expected value			N/A	N/A	*0.592*	*0.592*	*0.072*	*0.037*	*5.3*	
	Direct pour (no autosampler)	Test of lab accuracy	SRS, high	N/A	N/A	1.03	0.732	0.127	0.061	6.2	
	Expected value			N/A	N/A	*0.986*	*0.986*	*0.156*	*0.051*	*5.9*	
	Autosampler	Test of initial cleaning	DI blank	1	N/A	<0.01	<0.05	<0.025	<0.005	<0.25	
				2		<0.01	<0.05	<0.025	**0.00**	<0.25	
				3		<0.01	<0.05	<0.025	**0.00**	<0.25	
	Median					*<0.01*	*<0.05*	*<0.025*	*0.007*	*<0.25*	
	Standard Deviation					*0.000*	*0.000*	*0.000*	*0.004*	*0.0*	
	Autosampler	Establish dirty tubing	Water + dirt	1	61	0.299	0.837	0.306	0.139	3.6	Quantity of dirt undefined. Sampled from bucket, mixed by hand.
				2	57	0.297	0.976	0.301	0.132	3.6	
				3	48	0.299	0.96	0.294	0.133	3.6	
	Median				*57*	*0.299*	*0.96*	*0.301*	*0.133*	*3.6*	
	Standard Deviation				*6.7*	*0.001*	*0.076*	*0.006*	*0.004*	*0.0*	
	Autosampler	Test of cross contamination	DI blank	1	<0.2	<0.01	**0.0**	<0.025	<0.005	<0.25	Tests carryover from high TSS samples in Test 5.
				2	<0.2	<0.01	<0.05	<0.025	<0.005	<0.25	
				3	N/A	<0.01	<0.05	<0.025	<0.005	<0.25	
	Median				*<0.2*	*<0.01*	*<0.05*	*<0.025*	*<0.005*	*<0.25*	
	Standard Deviation				*0.0*	*0.000*	*0.032*	*0.000*	*0.000*	*0.0*	
	Autosampler	Test of dilution	SRS, high	1	N/A	1.02	0.943	0.141	0.053	6.2	Tests high SRS and possibility of dilution when sampling low concentration sources before high concentration sources.
				2		1.02	0.947	0.138	0.054	6.2	
				3		1.04	0.964	0.143	0.055	6.2	
	Expected value					*0.986*	*0.986*	*0.156*	*0.051*	*5.9*	
	Median					*1.02*	*0.947*	*0.141*	*0.054*	*6.2*	
	Standard Deviation					*0.012*	*0.011*	*0.003*	*0.001*	*0.0*	
	Autosampler	Test of cross contamination	SRS, low	1	N/A	0.616	0.591	0.069	0.039	5.6	Tests low SRS and possibility of cross contamination when sampling high-concentration sources before low concentration sources.
				2		0.62	0.609	0.069	0.039	5.6	
				3		0.626	0.603	0.068	0.045	5.6	
	Expected value					*0.592*	*0.592*	*0.072*	*0.037*	*5.3*	
	Median					*0.62*	*0.603*	*0.069*	*0.039*	*5.6*	
	Standard Deviation					*0.005*	*0.009*	*0.001*	*0.003*	*0.0*	

For the most part, results from the synthetic standard samples were within expected ranges. However, TKN concentrations in the low- and high-level synthetic standard samples (tests 2 and 3) seemed to be biased low by about 25 to 50 percent and the TP concentration in the high-level synthetic standard (Test 3) was almost 20 percent lower than expected. The synthetic standard tests were not repeated for this study, but they are repeated monthly as part of an ongoing quality-assurance program between the USGS and Clean Water Services. For 2002–03, TKN analysis of synthetic standard and spiked river water samples by Clean Water Services consistently had recoveries of 90–100 percent compared to expected values, indicating that the low recoveries for TKN shown in table 3 were anomalous. For TP, recoveries from the USGS-Clean Water Services Quality Assurance program during 2002–03 tended to be lower than for TKN, about 80–90 percent, but also were relatively consistent.

For field deployments of autosamplers, the determination of cross-section coefficients (also known as a box coefficient) is used to evaluate how point concentrations derived from an autosampler compare to depth- and width-integrated samples from across the range of streamflow conditions at the site (G.D. Glysson, U.S. Geological Survey, written commun., 2009). The coefficients also can be used to make corrections to autosampler data, if necessary. The box coefficient is calculated as the C_i/C_p, where C_i is a concentration derived from depth- and width-integrated sampling techniques, and C_p is the concentration from a pumping sampler. If the cross-section coefficient is near 1 for a given hydrologic condition, then no adjustment in concentrations is advised.

Box coefficients and carryover through autosampling were assessed at base flow in Fanno Creek through a comparison of replicate stream-water samples collected using the autosampler, with samples collected using depth- and width-integrating techniques according to USGS protocols (table 4). An additional comparison was completed at Dairy Creek during mid-winter storm sampling.

Some minor variations were observed in the determinations of autosampler box coefficients, but these were within analytical uncertainty. For example, the calculated box coefficient for TSS at Fanno Creek is 0.75; however, upon closer examination this primarily may be a result of laboratory variability. The triplicate cross-sectional samples (taken as aliquots from a churn splitter from a single depth- and width-integrated sampling) had moderate variation in the reported laboratory TSS concentrations (standard deviation 2.5), resulting in a median total TSS of 3 mg/L, whereas the replicate autosampler values were identical at a similar concentration (4 mg/L). *E. coli* bacteria counts showed the largest variability and the lowest box coefficient; however, bacteria counts also are known for their variability using current techniques and the differences shown here are not of concern at the low levels observed. Similarly, results of autosampler and equal width increment samples at Dairy Creek during a storm sampling in November 2003 were within 8 percent for all constituents and are indistinguishable from analytical variability. Adjustment of autosampler data by the box coefficient is not warranted by data in table 4 or by comparison with laboratory analytical uncertainty. However, additional comparisons at higher discharge (and higher suspended sediment concentrations) still are warranted to verify these findings under varying conditions and at different sampling sites.

To further evaluate carryover, the streambed was stirred to suspend sediments upstream of the autosampler intake, and samples were collected from within that plume and after the plume had passed or settled (approximately 15 minutes), as turbidity at the monitor returned to its baseline value. As expected, samples from the period when the streambed was being disturbed (sequence numbers 8–10, table 4) showed a high degree of variability, which is not a concern because the disturbance was essentially random. More importantly, after settling samples for all constituents (sequence numbers 11–13, table 4) were not much different from those prior to the disturbance of the streambed.

Table 4. Quality-assurance tests comparing samples collected using the autosampler with samples collected using depth- and width-integrating techniques, and testing carryover between sequential samples, Fanno and Dairy Creeks, Oregon.

[The cross-section coefficient (or box coefficient) is determined as C_i/C_p, where C_p is the concentration from the pumping sampler and C_i is the integrated, cross sectional concentration, collected according to U.S. Geological Survey sampling protocols. **Abbreviations:** *E. coli, Escherichia coli* bacteria; AS, autosampler; Rep, replicate; FC, Fanno Creek near Durham; EWI, equal width increment; DI, distilled, deionized water; DC, Dairy Creek at Highway 8; <, less than; E, estimated; mg/L, milligram per liter; N, nitrogen; P, phosphorus; mL, milliliter]

Description and time of sample collection	Test sequence No.	Location, date	Total suspended solids (mg/L)	Ammonium-nitrogen (mg/L as N)	Total Kjeldahl nitrogen (mg/L as N)	Nitrate (mg/L as N)	Total phosphorus (mg/L as P)	Soluble reactive phosphorus (mg/L as P)	Chloride (mg/L)	E. coli (colonies per 100 mL)	Comments
AS, Native Rep No. 1 11:30	1	FC, 06-06-2002	4	0.037	0.310	0.545	0.126	0.086	13.0	270	Native
AS, Native Rep No. 2 11:35	2		4	0.036	0.247	0.537	0.123	0.082	13.1	390	
Median (C_p)			*4*	*0.037*	*0.279*	*0.541*	*0.125*	*0.084*	*13.1*	*330*	
Standard Deviation			*0*	*0.001*	*0.045*	*0.005*	*0.002*	*0.003*	*0.071*	*84.9*	
EWI, Native Rep No. 1, 11:40	4	FC, 06-06-2002	6	0.040	0.279	0.547	0.128	0.079	13.3	190	Comparison of autosampler with equal-width-increment sample
EWI, Native Rep No. 2, 11:40	5		1	0.041	0.311	0.544	0.131	0.086	13.3	230	
EWI, Native Rep No. 3, 11:40	6		3	0.040	0.291	0.542	0.127	0.081	13.3	240	
Median (C_i)			*3*	*0.040*	*0.291*	*0.544*	*0.128*	*0.081*	*13.3*	*230*	
Standard Deviation			*2.5*	*0.001*	*0.016*	*0.002*	*0.002*	*0.004*	*0.000*	*26.5*	
Cross-section coefficient			*0.75*	*1.10*	*1.04*	*1.01*	*1.03*	*0.96*	*1.02*	*0.70*	
AS, DI Blank, after Natives, 11:45	7	FC, 06-06-2002	1	<0.01	<0.05	0.008	<0.025	<0.005	<0.25	<1	Test for carryover
AS, Kicked up turbidity, Rep No. 1, 12:00	8	FC, 06-06-2002	76	0.035	0.474	0.544	0.204	0.084	13.2	240	Tests dilution (from DI blank in sample 7)
AS, Kicked up turbidity, Rep No. 2, 12:02	9		147	0.036	0.452	0.542	0.276	0.084	13.2	330	
AS, Kicked up turbidity, Rep No. 3, 12:05	10		28	0.035	0.287	0.539	0.152	0.085	13.1	190	
Median			*76*	*0.035*	*0.452*	*0.542*	*0.204*	*0.084*	*13.2*	*240*	
Standard Deviation			*59.9*	*0.001*	*0.102*	*0.003*	*0.062*	*0.003*	*0.058*	*70.9*	
AS, Settled turbidity, 12:14	11	FC, 06-06-2002	5	0.035	0.19	0.543	0.117	0.081	13.2	260	Test for carryover
AS, Settled turbidity, 12:15	12		3	0.034	0.312	0.545	0.127	0.077	13.3	250	
AS, Settled turbidity, 12:16	13		5	0.035	0.268	0.542	0.125	0.081	13.5	360	
Median			*5*	*0.035*	*0.268*	*0.543*	*0.125*	*0.081*	*13.3*	*260*	
Standard Deviation			*1.2*	*0.001*	*0.062*	*0.001*	*0.005*	*0.002*	*0.153*	*60.8*	
AS, Native Water, 11:26	14	DC, 11-20-2003	13.0	E 0.018	0.478	0.700	0.144	0.052	6.42	190	Calculation of C_p at Dairy Creek
EWI, Native Water, 11:30	15		12.0	E 0.017	0.501	0.702	0.151	0.055	6.43	180	
Cross-section coefficient			*0.92*	*0.94*	*1.05*	*1.00*	*1.05*	*1.06*	*1.00*	*0.95*	

Clean Water Services Laboratory

Autosampler-derived water samples were analyzed by Clean Water Services at their water-quality laboratory in Hillsboro, Oregon. Samples were delivered immediately after retrieval from the autosamplers and subsampled for the indicated constituents (table 5). The analyzed constituents consisted of nutrients, suspended solids, bacteria, and chloride, several of which are regulated by the TMDL (Oregon Department of Environmental Quality, 2001). *E. coli* bacteria were analyzed immediately upon sample delivery to the Clean Water Services laboratory. Analyses for total and dissolved nutrients and TSS were started within 1–3 days of sample delivery, well within allowable holding times. Analytical methods and reporting limits are indicated in table 5.

Laboratory Quality Assurance

The Clean Water Services water-quality laboratory has a rigorous internal quality-assurance program. The laboratory also participates in the USGS national Standard Reference Sample (SRS) program, a national interlaboratory comparison study (see http://bqs.usgs.gov/srs/). Results from many years of participation in the SRS program have shown that the Clean Water Services laboratory consistently produces results that are sufficiently accurate for the parameters in this and other studies (bacteria are not included in the SRS). During 2002–05, Clean Water Services laboratory results for TP samples across a broad range of nominal concentrations (0.085–1.35 mg/L) were biased low by about -2 to -8 percent in 13 of 17 samples, and biased high by about 0 to 5 percent in 4 samples. Likewise, results from the TKN samples were biased low by about -1.5 to -16 percent in 8 of 10 samples, and

biased slightly high (as much as 2.5 percent) in the remainder. Furthermore, the Clean Water Services laboratory methods and protocols have been reviewed by the USGS Branch of Quality Systems and were determined to be suitable. The Clean Water Services laboratory also participates in an annual Tualatin River basin Interlaboratory Comparison Study, which includes all laboratories that routinely analyze water samples for government agencies in the Tualatin River basin.

On the basis of standard samples from both the Oregon Water Science Center (ORWSC) and national programs, TP data from Clean Water Services used in this study most likely were biased slightly low, but generally were consistent. The data, therefore, were unadjusted and considered adequate for the purposes of the study. When data from USGS and Clean Water Services laboratories are used together, any potential differences are reflected in the statistical uncertainty for the individual correlations. Ultimately, TKN was not included in the regression analysis, and any potential bias therefore was not relevant to the results of the study.

Field methods in use by Clean Water Services are similar to those used by USGS, including the collection of samples using depth- and width-integrating techniques and the use of churn splitters for subsampling; therefore, the respective laboratory methods are the most likely sources of any differences between the two datasets. Previous studies (Horowitz and others, 1994; Gray and others, 2000) have demonstrated that analysis of total suspended solids (TSS), the analytical technique used by Clean Water Services and many other agencies, is often biased low compared to the analysis for suspended sediment concentration (SSC), as practiced by USGS. The difference in results between the methods is primarily attributed to subsampling; specifically,

Table 5. Constituents analyzed from water samples collected during stormflows, Tualatin River tributaries, Oregon, May 2002 to September 2004.

[**Method number:** EPA, U S Environmental Protection Agency (1993); SM, Standard Methods (American Public Health Association, 1992) **Abbreviations:** STORET, U S Environmental Protection Agency's data Storage and Retrieval system; *E. coli, Escherichia coli*; mg/L, milligram per liter; mL, milliliter]

Parameter (abbreviation)	STORET code	Units	Method number	Reporting level	Analyzing laboratory
Total suspended solids (TSS)	530	mg/L	EPA 160.2	0.2	Clean Water Services
Ammonia nitrogen (NH_3-N)	608	mg/L	EPA 350.1	0.01	Clean Water Services
Total Kjeldahl nitrogen (TKN)	625	mg/L	EPA 351.2	0.1	Clean Water Services
Nitrate plus nitrite nitrogen (NO_3-N)	631	mg/L	EPA 353.1	0.01	Clean Water Services
Total phosphorus (TP)	665	mg/L	EPA 365.4	0.025	Clean Water Services
Soluble reactive phosphorus (SRP)	671	mg/L	EPA 365.1	0.005	Clean Water Services
Chloride (Cl$^-$)	941	mg/L	EPA 300.3 A	0.1	Clean Water Services
E. coli bacteria	31648	$(100\ mL)^{-1}$	SM 9213 D	1	Clean Water Services

the SSC method includes measurement of sediment in the entire sample, but the TSS method measures sediment amounts in a subsample removed from the original sample bottle. The subsampling process can underestimate sediment concentrations, especially if sand concentrations are high or flocculation occurs, because these particles settle quickly in a sample bottle, and obtaining a representative subsample is difficult (Gray and others, 2000). No data are available for direct comparison of SSC and TSS in the USGS and Clean Water Services databases, respectively. For this report, the TSS and SSC data were combined without adjustment, and the variability introduced by the two methods is therefore incorporated into the regression results.

Data Aggregation

The intent of this report is to use the available datasets for model development and calibration, and to compare the most promising model forms and their resulting coefficients, to determine the likelihood that suitable predictive models can be used to understand transport and loading of the indicated constituents (TSS, TP, *E. coli* bacteria) at the Fanno and Dairy Creek sites. The data were aggregated into data scenarios, to evaluate (1) model calibration using the autosampler-only dataset, and model validation using available Clean Water Services data; (2) model calibration with the autosampler data plus the available historical USGS data, and model validation with Clean Water Services data; and (3) a combined dataset using data from all sources for calibration, while retaining independent data for model validation. Details of these scenarios for Fanno Creek at Durham are shown in table 6 and figure 3. During the model construction process, if the input variables identified as contributing the most information remained similar regardless of the scenario used, and likewise if the regression coefficient values remained moderately consistent for a given predicted variable regardless of scenario, then it could be concluded that the models were relatively robust and could be used reliably until additional data are collected that can be used to refine those models. On the other hand, if the use of different datasets resulted in widely varying model forms and coefficients, or goodness-of-fit diagnostic statistics that differ greatly, then additional and targeted data most likely are needed prior to development of useful models. All independent variables (specific conductance and turbidity data plus streamflow or stage) were consistently taken from the same data sources for all scenarios and model runs. Data from continuous monitors came from USGS, and streamflow or stage data came from USGS for Fanno Creek and from OWRD for Dairy Creek at Highway 8.

Duration curves are commonly used in hydrologic studies to document the range of conditions measured at a site during an indicated period, including the frequency

and magnitude of certain conditions. These curves depict cumulative distributions of all measurements during the study period, and show the percentage of time during the study period that specific values for the constituent were equaled or exceeded. Although typically used for discharge records, duration curves have increasingly been constructed for water quality constituents for which high density data can be collected, including continuous monitoring data such as those collected in this study (Rasmussen and others, 2008). Duration curves (fig. 3) for selected continuous parameters used in the regressions provide information about the relative magnitude of the parameter values during sampling, compared to the full range measured at the site during the study period. For example, if a given turbidity associated with a particular sample was exceeded only 5 percent of the time during the study period, then that measurement represents a relatively high turbidity; however, if the turbidity of a sample was exceeded 50 percent of the time or more often, then that sample represents average or low-flow conditions, respectively.

During the early phases of model development, it was determined that exclusive use of the autosampler-derived data (Scenario 1) to construct predictive statistical models was flawed because of correlation issues. The regression process assumes that input data points are truly independent; however, data collected over a single hydrograph are not completely independent of one another. For example, as streamflow increases during a storm, samples collected sequentially are more likely to be similar to each other than samples collected during different storms or under completely different sampling conditions. This serial correlation is a problem when using the Scenario 1 (autosampler-only) dataset for model building purposes. Methods to account for serial correlation are available, such as introducing a lag in the data to reduce the interdependence of individual samples (Helsel and Hirsch, 1992); however, these methods were not used in this study because it was recognized that, whether or not a lag was introduced to account for serial correlation, the Scenario 1 datasets would be insufficient for regression modeling because the range of stream conditions encompassed by the autosampler deployments was limited (fig. 3A). As an example, the peak discharge sampled by the autosamplers at Fanno Creek was about 134 ft³/s (table 6); although discharges during the study period were as much as 780 ft³/s (fig. 3) and historical high flows occasionally have been greater than 1,000 ft³/s. For the purposes of simplicity and to focus on the larger study objectives, serial correlation was therefore ignored in the analysis of Scenario 1 and 2; instead, the Scenario 3 dataset was created to avoid serial correlation (see below). When appropriate, the potential influence of serial correlation on model development based on Scenario 1 and Scenario 2 is discussed.

Table 6. Datasets showing laboratory sample results and summary statistics for scenarios used for calibration and validation of regression models with continuous monitors at Fanno Creek, Durham, Oregon.

[Discharge, turbidity, and specific conductance data were from records at stream gages and continuous monitors. Occasional Clean Water Services samples were collected at higher discharges than shown here, but continuous monitors were not deployed at the time so samples could not be used for this study. Note that USGS uses suspended sediment concentration (SSC) rather than total suspended solids (TSS). SSC and TSS data were combined without adjustment for Scenario 2 and Scenario 3. **Abbreviations:** FNU, Formazin Nephelometric Unit; *n*, number of samples (numbers for individual models may vary where missing values or outliers were removed); NWIS, National Water Information System water quality database; USGS, U.S. Geological Survey; ft³/s, cubic foot per second; µS/cm, microsiemens per centimeter; mg/L, milligram per liter; No./100 mL, colony count per 100 milliliters]

Scenario and summary statistic	Calibration						Validation		
	Discharge (ft³/s)	Turbidity (FNU)	Specific conductance (µS/cm)	Total suspended solids (mg/L)	Total phosphorus (mg/L)	E. coli (No./100 mL)	Total suspended solids (mg/L)	Total phosphorus (mg/L)	E. coli (No./100 mL)
Scenario 1	Autosampler (2002–03), *n* = 54						Clean Water Services ambient monitoring (2001–04), *n* = 98		
Minimum	7.1	5.7	110.0	4.0	0.08	180	2.0	0.08	56
Maximum	134.4	131	245.0	196.0	0.47	10,000	260.0	0.60	12,000
Mean	65.7	47	159.5	51.0	0.19	2,829	16.9	0.15	763
Median	63.9	38	146.0	37.1	0.15	1,300	7.2	0.14	325
Standard deviation	31.0	30	34.7	45.6	0.10	3,174	34.8	0.08	2,020
Scenario 2	Autosampler (2002–03) + USGS NWIS (2001–07), *n* = 131						Clean Water Services ambient monitoring (2001–04), *n* = 98		
Minimum	1.12	1.4	63.8	0.5	0.08	180	2.0	0.08	56
Maximum	505.0	131	394.0	242.0	0.47	10,000	260.0	0.60	12,000
Mean	49.1	28	187.2	29.9	0.15	2,829	16.9	0.15	763
Median	33.2	17	182.2	12.5	0.14	1,300	7.2	0.14	325
Standard deviation	65.0	29	52.7	40.9	0.07	3,174	34.8	0.08	2,020
Scenario 3	Autosampler peak discharge samples, USGS NWIS high flow 2001–07, Clean Water Services first monthly + high flow, *n* = 96						Autosampler non-peak discharge samples, USGS non-high flow, Clean Water Services remaining monthly and non-high flow, *n* = 80		
Minimum	1.1	3.9	63.8	2.0	0.08	67	0.5	0.08	56
Maximum	505.0	131	281.0	242.0	0.47	6,300	260.0	0.60	10,000
Mean	57.9	25	177.5	26.3	0.14	824	29.6	0.17	1,565
Median	35.4	17	168.0	13.5	0.13	345	10.0	0.14	520
Standard deviation	80.7	26	48.8	39.4	0.05	1,428	40.7	0.09	2,546

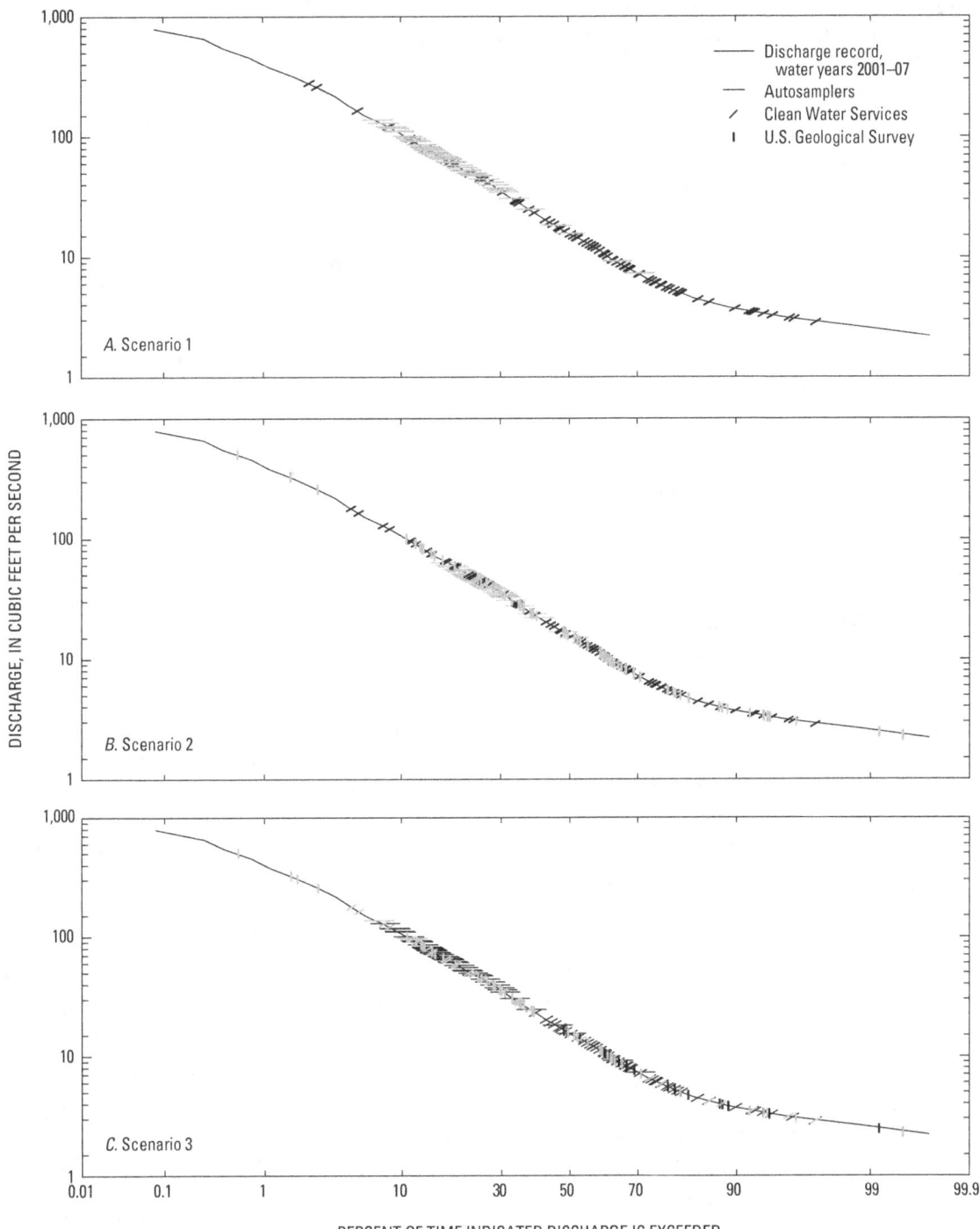

Figure 3. Flow duration curves with samples collected from each data source for (*A*) Scenario 1, (*B*) Scenario 2, and (*C*) Scenario 3, for Fanno Creek near Durham, Oregon, water years 2001–07. Samples used for model calibration are in orange, and samples used for model validation are in black. See table 6 for a description of the data aggregation into Scenarios 1, 2, and 3.

In Scenario 2, Fanno Creek autosampler data are augmented with additional data collected by the USGS for water years 2001-07 (table 6 and fig. 3B); validation is done with Clean Water Services data as in Scenario 1. Scenario 2 provides an example of one relatively simple method to aggregate data when multiple sources are available. Serial correlation between autosampler-derived data remains an issue in Scenario 2, although the influence of serial correlation on the outcome is reduced by the additional data. USGS data were collected for various purposes, including routine monitoring (USGS National Water-Quality Assessment Program, http://water.usgs.gov/nawqa/) and other, more targeted studies (McCarthy, 2000; Anderson and Rounds, 2003), and are stored in the USGS National Water Information System (NWIS) database (http://nwis.waterdata.usgs.gov/or/nwis/qwdata). The USGS and Clean Water Services routine monitoring designs do not target specific flow conditions, and the resulting dataset is primarily composed of base-flow (non-storm) samples during all months; high-flow samples are present only when storm events coincided with scheduled sampling events. At least one USGS study (Anderson and Rounds, 2003) did focus on high-flow and runoff conditions, thus providing several samples at discharges greater than those sampled by the deployed autosamplers. Additionally, occasional USGS and Clean Water Services samples were collected prior to 2002 at higher discharges, but continuous monitors were not deployed at the time so the results could not be used for this study.

Scenario 3 was created specifically to minimize the stated problems in the Scenario 1 and 2 datasets. To avoid the serial correlation bias, Scenario 3 used only the autosampler data collected during peak flow in each individual storm sampled (that is, one sample per storm); to minimize base-flow bias, a subset of the routine Clean Water Services ambient monitoring data was used with selected high-flow data from the USGS and Clean Water Services historical datasets. From the routine Clean Water Services data, only the first data point in each month was included, which reduced the number of base-flow samples but still represented seasonal patterns; sometimes these samples represented moderate storm runoff, although most samples were collected at relatively low flows. For high flow, any samples that were potentially representative of storm response were desired; thus, high flow was determined as any data point with an associated discharge greater than the 25th percentile value for that month, as defined from monthly flow-duration statistics computed from the NWIS database for the period of record at Fanno Creek near Durham (USGS stream-gaging station 14206950), October 2000–September 2007. This strategy allowed Scenario 3 to capture summer and spring storm responses while minimizing samples corresponding to low flows. Because of the paucity of high-flow samples, most available samples were used for calibration; however, a few were retained for validation (fig. 3C).

For Scenario 1, the highest discharges sampled for model calibration were exceeded about 10 percent of the time from water year 2001 to 2007 (fig. 3). The Scenario 1 validation dataset (in black) has three samples at slightly higher discharges (exceeded about 7–9 percent of the time). By far the bulk of the samples were at discharges exceeded about 10–70 percent of the time, during base-flow to moderate storm runoff. The addition of data from USGS in Scenario 2, and re-aggregation to use a broad range of the samples from Clean Water Services' database in Scenario 3, added successively greater numbers of samples from higher discharges, or those exceeded less than 1 to about 10 percent of the time. However, even in Scenario 3 only a few of these higher flow samples were available, and some were needed for model validation, whereas in each scenario large numbers of samples were collected during relatively low-flow conditions, when the respective discharges were frequently exceeded.

Any potential contamination detected during the autosampler quality-assurance tests (table 3) was well below most of the sample concentrations included in the aggregated datasets. For example, although soluble reactive phosphorus was detected in blank water at 0.007–0.009 mg/L, the minimum TP concentrations in Scenarios 1, 2, and 3 were 0.08 mg/L, and the medians ranged from 0.13 to 0.15 mg/L (table 6). Maximum ambient concentrations for model calibration were as much as 0.47 mg/L. Even if contamination at less than 0.01 mg/L is pervasive, its effect on the model formulation is likely small.

For the site at Dairy Creek near Highway 8, data were similarly aggregated into scenarios; however, no historical, independent data from USGS were available, so only two scenarios were evaluated. These and other differences in the input data are described in the section on Dairy Creek model results. Duration curves for samples used in the Dairy Creek analysis are not shown because the Dairy Creek data aggregation process was less complex than for Fanno Creek, and potential problems with backwater effects on discharge would complicate the construction of duration curves.

Dairy Creek at Highway 8 is sampled routinely by Clean Water Services but not by USGS, with the exception of the autosampler deployments in autumn 2003. For that reason, the available data for calibration and validation of regression models from 2002 to 2004 are more limited than at Fanno Creek (table 7). Scenario 1 was derived in the same way as for Fanno Creek, using the autosampler data for calibration and Clean Water Services data for validation. However, for calibration, Scenario 2 used the Clean Water Services samples at high stage, the first routine Clean Water Services samples from each month, and the peak discharge samples collected from the two autosamplers during autumn storms.

Table 7. Datasets showing laboratory sample results and summary statistics for scenarios used for calibration and validation of regression models with continuous monitors at Dairy Creek at Highway 8 near Hillsboro, Oregon.

[Discharge, turbidity, and specific conductance data were from records at stream gages and continuous monitors. Occasional Clean Water Services samples were collected at higher discharges than shown here, but continuous monitors were not installed at the time so samples could not be used for this study. **Abbreviations:** FNU, Formazin Nephelometric Unit; *E. coli*, *Escherichia coli* bacteria; *n*, number of samples (numbers for individual models may vary where missing values or outliers were removed); ft³/s, cubic foot per second; μS/cm, microsiemens per centimeter; mg/L, milligram per liter; No./100 mL, colony count per 100 milliliters]

Scenario and summary statistic	Calibration						Validation		
	Discharge (ft³/s)	Turbidity (FNU)	Specific conductance (μS/cm)	Total suspended solids (mg/L)	Total phosphorus (mg/L)	*E. coli* (No./100 mL)	Total suspended solids (mg/L)	Total phosphorus (mg/L)	*E. coli* (No./100 mL)
Scenario 1	Autosampler (2002–03), *n* = 38						Clean Water Services ambient monitoring (2001–04), *n* = 116		
Minimum	38.7	5.7	117.0	5.0	0.09	40	2.8	0.05	28
Maximum	158.7	30	141.0	31.0	0.23	950	38.0	0.29	1,800
Mean	90.6	14	127.9	13.3	0.14	331	11.9	0.12	286
Median	92.4	15	124.5	11.5	0.14	260	11.2	0.11	185
Standard deviation	34.7	6	7.2	6.7	0.04	256	5.4	0.04	302
Scenario 2	Autosampler peak discharge samples, Clean Water Services first monthly + high flow, *n* = 42						Autosampler non-peak discharge samples, Clean Water Services remaining monthly and non-high flow, *n* = 113		
Minimum	16.0	3.2	67.0	2.8	0.06	28	2.8	0.05	31
Maximum	705.0	16.2	190.0	38.0	0.21	1,500	31.0	0.29	1,800
Mean	137.1	10.0	108.3	12.8	0.11	256	12.1	0.13	314
Median	74.8	9.6	102.0	12.4	0.11	110	11.2	0.13	225
Standard deviation	162.2	3.4	25.8	6.4	0.04	329	5.5	0.04	277

Validation data for Scenario 2 used the remaining Clean Water Services monitoring data combined with the autosampler data from times other than peak discharge. This formulation of Scenario 2 datasets differs from Scenario 2 used for Fanno Creek (table 6), where USGS data along with the autosampler data were used for calibration in Scenario 2. Furthermore, no Scenario 3 dataset was warranted for Dairy Creek.

Having minimized the potential serial correlation and base-flow bias problems, the Scenario 3 dataset from Fanno Creek is presumed the most likely to produce robust regression models. This dataset includes high-flow data from USGS, monthly and high-flow data from Clean Water Services, and the peak discharge samples collected by the autosamplers. Two major limitations in the compilation of data, however, result from using historical data rather than data collected specifically for this study. First, few samples were collected during storm and high-flow conditions, which not only reduces the size and range of the available dataset for model calibration but also the available data for model validation. Second, for the purposes of this exercise, laboratory data from all sources were compiled together.

Regression Models

Several methods were used to evaluate potential regression models, with the intent that any models described herein are examples of the types of models that could be useful for predictive purposes, even if they currently lack sufficient data for either calibration or validation purposes. The functional form of the models is

$$y = f(x_1, x_2, \dots x_n), \tag{1}$$

where

y is the dependent variable,
$x_1, x_2, \dots x_n$ are explanatory variables, and
the notation
$f()$ indicates that y is a function of the indicated explanatory variables.

If initial correlation attempts look promising, then the results are given in tables for a specified parameter that show model coefficients and regression statistics for regression equations of the form:

$$y = ax_1 + bx_2 + \dots mx_n + \varepsilon, \tag{2}$$

where

$a, b, \dots m$ are regression coefficients,
ε is an error term, or intercept, and
$y, x_1, x_2, \dots x_n$ are as already described.

The dependent variables (y) are the predicted concentrations of water-quality constituents from laboratory analysis, such as TSS, TP, or *E. coli* bacteria, and the independent or explanatory variables are the continuously measured data such as streamflow, stage, specific conductance, or turbidity. Residual plots were generated during the regression process (SAS Institute, 1989) to help determine the degree of homoscedasticity (homogeneity in the variance) and identify outliers in the datasets.

Log transformation, which sometimes allows more robust regression predictions, was performed on independent and dependent variables and these transformed variables were evaluated for utility in making predictions. Log transformation can provide better homoscedasticity and result in more symmetric datasets with normal residuals (Gray and others, 2000). When regression models are developed with data that violate assumptions of normality and homoscedasticity, the models are less likely to apply over the range of expected conditions for the site, and large prediction errors may occur. Rasmussen and others (2009) recommend log transformations for development of estimated suspended sediment concentrations and loads as a function of continuous turbidity and (or) discharge data, and this approach has been used with success for suspended sediment and other selected variables in streams in Kansas (Rasmussen and others, 2008), Oregon (Uhrich and Bragg, 2003; Anderson, 2007), and Florida (Lietz and Debiak, 2005).

Some constituents may be affected by seasonal considerations that explicitly need to be included in the regression modeling. For example, nutrient concentrations in surface waters might be partially dependent on water temperature and its effects on biological processes, riparian plant growth and its ability to reduce erosion, or even the amount of daylight hours and its effects on algal production. Similarly, bacterial growth in streams (*E. coli* bacteria, in this study) is generally considered tightly coupled with water temperature, among other factors. Even TSS could have a seasonal component if factors such as the effect of riparian vegetation on erosion or seasonal rainfall patterns are important. Although the continuously measured parameters used in this study (discharge, turbidity, specific conductance) inherently incorporate these seasonal fluctuations, seasonality was also explored in the regression modeling with sine and cosine transformations of the sample date. The following two terms were evaluated as additional explanatory variables:

$$c * \sin(date * 2 * \text{pi} / 365.25), \text{ and}$$
$$d * \cos(date * 2 * \text{pi} / 365.25),$$

where

c and d are regression coefficients similar to a, b, and m in equation 2, and
$date$ is in decimal days of the year, with 365.25 representing the average number of days in a year.

These two terms must be used together to capture and express an annual periodic cycle with an unknown phase offset. Using only the sine or cosine term without the offset is less likely to capture a periodic signal in the data. However, the sine and cosine terms also could cause an interaction with the other independent variables; therefore, the model building is done with and without the sine and cosine terms, and the presence of such interactions is then detected using an F-test (Helsel and Hirsch, 1992; R. Hirsch, U.S. Geological Survey, written commun., December 2008). Sine and cosine terms were tested in regression models for TSS, TP, and *E. coli* bacteria for the data scenarios that are presumed the most robust input calibration data at the respective sites; that is, Scenario 3 for Fanno Creek and Scenario 2 for Dairy Creek.

Data used in this study were initially examined graphically for patterns between potential explanatory variables and the dependent variables. Some patterns that were observed included the presence of bimodal distributions or possible outliers that might affect regressions among the constituents, and correlations (either positive or negative) that might be indicative of predictive signals. Because of their potentially large effect on the regression statistics, outliers were defined as any data points lying more than three times the interquartile range beyond the 25th and 75th percentile values for a particular constituent (Lewis, 1996; Uhrich and Bragg, 2003; Lietz and Debiak, 2005; Rasmussen and others, 2008), and investigated for possible data coding problems, field or laboratory irregularities, or other documented issues that might explain their abnormality. If documented problems could not be corrected, the data were excluded from regression calculations, whereas the data were retained if all available information confirmed the sample integrity.

Model building was initially performed with backward, stepwise, linear regressions (Helsel and Hirsch, 1992; SAS Institute, 1989), with an alpha value of 0.05, using either the original or log-transformed data, whichever provided the best fit. When stepwise-regression selected independent variables that were surrogates for each other (for example, untransformed and log-transformed versions of the same variable, or stage and streamflow), one variable was removed and the stepwise process was repeated. However, stepwise regression algorithms tend to continue adding explanatory variables until the coefficient of determination (R^2) is maximized, whether or not the added variables actually provide useful information, and can create models that are overfitted (Burnham and Anderson, 2002). Therefore, the initial stepwise regressions were used only as a starting point to evaluate additional model forms using reduced sets of explanatory variables. Subsequent iterations were performed to minimize Mallow's Cp (SAS Institute, 1989; Draper and

Smith, 1998), and used the adjusted-R^2, which penalizes additional variables, as a model selection scheme. This process was similar to a "Best-Subsets" regression (Draper and Smith, 1998), although less formal.

One challenge when using stepwise regression or other algorithms to select the best correlation was exploring the use of variables in their native units and log transformed forms. Although one might want to evaluate native and transformed variables, inclusion of the forms together introduces opportunities for significant cross correlation or multicollinearity; software programs that automatically perform such algorithms are usually incapable of distinguishing between variables that are truly independent and those that are transformed versions of another variable. The process of model selection by necessity, therefore, was iterative and ultimately was reduced to using log-transformed dependent variables to minimize the possibility that the resulting predicted values would be negative, while evaluating native and transformed versions of the independent variables using the methods discussed previously.

Interactions between independent variables, such as occurs if one variable is dependent on another, can reduce the reliability of correlation coefficients (Draper and Smith, 1998), and can contribute to overfitting of regression models (SAS Institute, 1989). The net result tends to be an increase in the standard errors of the independent variables, an effect that is minimized with increased observations. One measure of multicollinearity is the Variance Inflation Factor (VIF), which measures the degree to which the variance of the coefficient of determination for a particular variable is increased because of interdependence between that variable and others in a particular model. The VIF is calculated as

$$1/(1-R_1^2)\,, \tag{3}$$

where

R_1^2 is the coefficient of determination for the regression of the *i*th independent variable on all other independent variables (Draper and Smith, 1998).

The value of the VIFs are dependent solely on the interactions of the independent variables with each other. Thus, VIFs for a set of independent variables can vary according to datasets used, or in this study, according to scenarios. Likewise, the same dataset may be used in regressions for different dependent variables, and the VIFs would be identical for each identical grouping of independent variables; regressions with only one variable have no interactions and, therefore, no VIF is applicable.

The acceptable magnitude of a VIF is dependent on the objectives of a specific study. Several rules-of-thumb for VIFs are sometimes given, and tend to range from greater than 0.2 to less than 10 (Helsel and Hirsch; SAS Institute), but variables with VIFs exceeding these levels may still be useful in a model if they have a low p value. Alternately, a critical value for a maximum acceptable VIF (referred to hereafter as VIF_{crit}) for an equation can be calculated by substituting the overall coefficient of determination of the model (R^2, or in this study, adjusted-R^2) for R_i^2 in equation 3 (SAS Institute, 1989). If the result is smaller than any of the VIFs of any variable in the equation, then multicollinearity may have contributed to the inclusion of that variable in the model, although consideration of the significance of that variable (p value) in the model remains important. A low adjusted-R^2, as in equation 3, will result in a low VIF_{crit} and reduce the apparent level of interaction that is allowed among model variables. In this study, VIFs were obtained as output from the statistical software (SAS Institute, 1989).

When log-transformed dependent variables are included in regression models, a transformation bias can be introduced when the results are converted back to native units for making predictions. In these cases, a bias correction factor, or BCF (Helsel and Hirsch, 1992) is necessary; the BCF is multiplied by the value of the predicted dependent variable after the BCF is transformed back into native units by taking the antilog. That is,

$$y' = BCF * 10^y, \qquad (4)$$

where

    y' is the final, predicted value, untransformed into
        native units, and

    y is the value of the log-transformed dependent
        variable as calculated in equation 2.

Duan's BCF is the average of the residuals of the dependent variable in the regression dataset; when the dependent variable was log transformed, the antilog of the residual was taken before averaging to determine the BCF. Likewise, when log-transformation was used for prediction, the lower and upper 95 percent prediction interval values (SAS Institute, 1989; Helsel and Hirsch, 1992) also were converted to native units with the antilog, and these were corrected using the same BCF as the predicted dependent variables.

For the Fanno Creek and Dairy Creek sites, predicted hourly concentrations and their 95 percent prediction intervals were computed for selected water-quality constituents using regression models, and using the indicated hourly monitor and streamflow records as independent variables. Predictions were evaluated against the available validation data (tables 6 and 7) by interpolating the hourly predictions to the time of the validation samples, and then comparing the resulting values to the validation samples using a series of goodness-of-fit statistics (table 8). This validation exercise for the regression models provides an independent measure of the quality of the predictions for the dependent variables and could assist in the decision about which model is the most robust. Not all goodness-of-fit metrics in table 8 are shown in subsequent tables of model results, due to space constraints, but all were used in evaluation of model performance. The available input datasets and resulting regression models were not adequate for making predictions for the non-target sites (table 1), and only the preferred model forms, without the supporting regression coefficients, are presented to provide an indication of the most important independent variables to consider for monitoring.

Where regression results seem to provide a reasonable starting point for future modeling, several model forms are shown along with their respective coefficients, diagnostic statistics, and selected goodness-of-fit statistics. Diagnostic statistics include the adjusted-R^2 and the root mean square error (RMSE) of the regression. The RMSE assesses the typical error between predicted and observed values. As the root mean square is equal to the square of the mean plus the square of the standard deviation, then if the mean error is zero (no bias), the RMSE is equal to the standard deviation of the errors. The Nash-Sutcliffe Coefficient (Nash and Sutcliffe, 1970), otherwise known as the Coefficient of Model-Fit Efficiency, is one of the goodness-of-fit statistics computed for these models and commonly is used for assessing the accuracy of hydrologic models. Imbalance in the model residuals is assessed by examining the number of negative and positive differences between a model's predicted results and the comparable laboratory values; a sign test can be used to estimate the likelihood that the residuals were random in the positive or negative directions.

Results using several models illustrate the potential explanatory variables and transformations of variables that could be used and the effects of using different input datasets. More detailed regression, neural network, or autoregressive models could be built and would be useful for comparison. This study, however, is meant to be a proof of concept rather than a definitive model building exercise. Simple multiple linear regressions should be sufficient to determine whether adequate information is present in the monitor data to predict TP, TSS, and *E. coli* bacteria in Fanno and Dairy Creeks.

Table 8. Goodness-of-fit statistics used for evaluation of regression model predictions.

[**Abbreviations:** NA, not applicable; n, number of samples]

Description of test	Acceptable range	Explanation
Number of points compared	NA; more points	Number of validation data points with comparable predicted values from the regression. Analogous to 'n' in regression model, determines degrees of freedom.
Mean error (ME)	Near zero—exact range depends on constituent	Average error between predicted values and laboratory values in validation data set—a good measure of bias.
Mean absolute relative error (percent)	0–50	Average absolute difference between predicted and laboratory value as normalized to laboratory values.
Root mean square error (RMSE)	Depends on constituent; a number closer to zero is better	A measure of the square of the mean plus the square of the standard deviation. If the mean error is zero, then the RMSE is equal to the standard deviation of the errors—a good measure of the magnitude of the typical error of the prediction. A high R^2 with a poor fit based on the RMSE is possible if the range of the data is large.
Coefficient of determination (R^2)	Approximately 0.6–1.0, although user defined.	Analogous to coefficient of determination for regression, based on differences of predicted and known values of independent variables.
Nash-Sutcliffe coefficient	Approximately 0.6–1.0, although user defined.	Also called the Coefficient of Model Fit Efficiency—it is the proportion of variance in the measured values that is explained by the predicted values, and is a more rigorous fit statistic than the coefficient of determination. A value of 1.0 is a perfect fit. A value of 0 indicates that the model predictions are only as accurate as the mean of the observed data. Anything less than zero means that the observed mean is a better predictor than the model. However, note that the value of this coefficient is highly dependent on the available validation data. If validation data are insufficient to characterize the response variable, this coefficient may under-represent the true fit of the model.
Number of negative differences	Similar to number of positive differences	Number of predicted values that are less than the relevant laboratory value.
Number of positive differences	Similar to number of negative differences	Number of predicted values that are greater than the relevant laboratory value.
Probability from sign test	> Typically greater than 0.05	Using the sign test on the residuals, this is the statistical probability that the number of positive and negative differences could have resulted if the errors were truly random in direction.
z-statistic from sign test	< Typically less than 1.96	Using the sign test on the residuals, the z-statistic provides a statistical measure that determines whether the number of positive and negative differences could have resulted if the errors were random in direction.

Relations Between Continuous Monitor Data and Selected Water-Quality Constituents

Autosampler Deployment Dates and Conditions

Streams were sampled with autosamplers during storms from spring 2002 through autumn 2003 (table 9). Because of differences in hydrologic characteristics and responses among sites, inconsistent spatial extent of storms, and resource availability, only a few streams were sampled during any individual storm. To obtain the desired number of samples (approximately 48–50) covering reasonably broad ranges of field parameters and to develop robust regression models, some streams were sampled during more storms than others. For example, Rock, Chicken, and Fanno Creeks were sampled during three storms each, whereas Gales Creek was only sampled during one storm.

In some cases, the storms sampled by autosamplers at individual sites represented different seasonal conditions. For example, Beaverton and Rock Creeks were both sampled in summer (June) and autumn (December). This difference in season helped increase the range of field and laboratory constituent values obtained, which ordinarily would be useful for deriving strong correlations. For some field values at some sites, however, the same temporal differences also resulted in bimodal distributions that likely reduced the quality of the autosampler-derived regression models. For example, specific conductance at some sites was less variable during individual storms than between seasons, which abnormally skewed regressions that relied on specific conductance at those sites. For this reason, where bimodal distributions were observed in the initial graphical analysis, those parameters were removed from consideration for regressions at the respective locations. For the most part, bimodal distributions occurred primarily at the non-target sites, whereas the autosampler deployments at Fanno Creek were primarily during late spring in 2002 and 2003, and the deployments at Dairy Creek occurred in autumn 2003 (table 9) possibly serving to narrow the resulting range of constituent values.

In the following sections, figures are provided to show the percentage of time during the study period that the field values measured during the autosampler deployments were exceeded. Monitors were installed primarily during the late spring, summer, and early autumn because of reduced access when winter flows were high. Therefore, the data used to determine the percentage of time a given value was exceeded do not include the typically higher-discharge in winter, when it could be expected that, on average, specific conductance generally would be lower but also highly variable, and turbidities would be higher than during the months of monitor deployment.

Table 9.   Dates of autosampling and peak storm discharges at Tualatin River tributary sites, Oregon, spring 2002 to autumn 2003.

[**Abbreviations:** ft^3/s, cubic feet per second]

Stream	Sampling dates	Peak storm discharge (ft^3/s)
Beaverton Creek	June 28–30, 2002	207
	December 10–12, 2002	207
Chicken Creek	June 17, 2003	12.2
	May 8, 2003	22
	May 17–18, 2003	27
Dairy Creek	October 9, 2003	42
	November 19–20, 2003	158
Fanno Creek	June 17–18, 2002	94
	May 4–5, 2003	134
	May 8–9, 2003	118
Gales Creek	November 17–20, 2003	245
Rock Creek	June 28–30, 2002	180
	December 10–12, 2002	372
	September 5–9, 2003	70

The Fanno and Dairy Creek sites were sampled during relatively moderate storms during the study period (fig. 3), resulting in a smaller but sometimes bimodal range for specific conductance and turbidity. Overall, the range of physical conditions encountered while sampling was somewhat narrow. Discharges increased moderately during storms but mostly did not represent the highest peaks that commonly occur during some years; likewise, turbidity and other field parameters showed only moderate ranges during the sampled storms. Caution must be exercised when using regression equations from this analysis if conditions are outside the range documented during this study (tables 6 and 7). Extrapolation of regression equations beyond the bounds of the data used to formulate them is considered a potentially large source of error and is not recommended (Helsel and Hirsch, 1992). To a certain extent, the validation datasets in this study allow evaluation of the error introduced when the regression models are applied to conditions beyond the range of the input datasets. However, the validation datasets are limited in the range of conditions encompassed and therefore do not provide much additional information about the adequacy of the regression models to address many of the higher flow conditions.

Fanno Creek at Durham Road

Autosampler Data

The storms were sampled by autosamplers at Fanno Creek in late spring or early summer. The sampled peak discharges (94–134 ft^3/s, table 9) covered a narrow range of potential discharges for this site (fig. 3); although storms of this size are fairly representative for May–June in most years, peak discharges exceeded these amounts at least 15 times on other dates during the study period (http://waterdata.usgs. gov/or/nwis/, accessed November 17, 2005). Fanno Creek is in a highly urbanized basin and responds quickly to rainfall making it a challenge to anticipate and react to storms to collect high-flow samples. This situation is indicative of the need for automatic sampling and increases the likelihood that extreme events will not be adequately sampled.

Several critical constituents exhibited less variability during individual autosampler storm events than between sampling events. This resulted in bimodal data distributions of the autosampler data, as illustrated for specific conductance, in figure 4. Data points tended to be clustered into small groups, and generally represented average conditions rather than the rarely occurring extremes usually indicative of storm conditions.

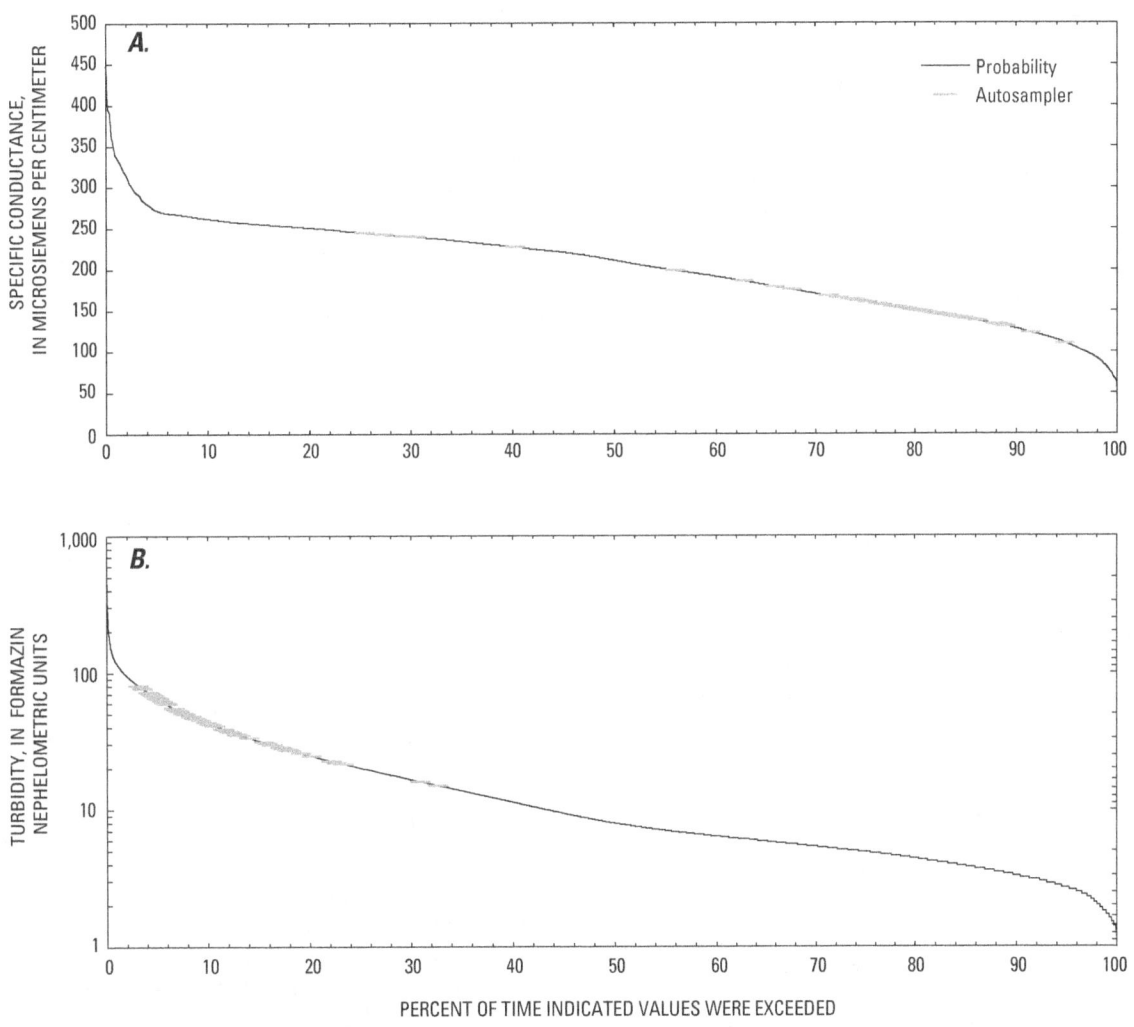

Figure 4.   Probability that (A) specific conductances and (B) turbidities during autosampling were exceeded at Fanno Creek at Durham, Oregon, May 2002 to September 2004.

Specific conductance measured during sample collection, for example, was exceeded from about 25 to more than 95 percent of the time during the study period. The duration curves for specific conductance are different than for turbidity because the sources and mechanisms affecting the two are different. During base flow, specific conductance at Fanno Creek is relatively high (>200 µS/cm) but rainfall is dilute (about 0–20 µS/cm) so dilution by rain can cause a large range in responses. Turbidity caused by suspended particles may come from upland sources transporting particles to the stream, or from within the stream from erosion or resuspension. Turbidity values measured during autosampler deployment were more indicative of the higher and more continuous range during the study than were specific conductances, and were exceeded only about 2 to 34 percent of the time during the entire study period. Model results from conditions of specific conductances, and turbidities beyond those actually measured during the samplings in the Scenario 1–3 datasets (table 6) cannot be verified.

The relations between Fanno Creek field parameters and laboratory sample results from the autosampler deployments and the Scenario 3 dataset show some useful patterns (fig. 5). In figure 5A, the symbols for a given storm and constituent combination sometimes show different patterns indicating the differences between storms. Possible linear relations for the autosampler dataset are indicated for combinations of turbidity or discharge with TSS, TP, and *E. coli* bacteria. In the larger dataset represented by Scenario 3, linear relations are indicated between turbidity and TSS, TP, and *E. coli* bacteria. Several other potential relations are indicated, particularly for discharge and TSS or TP; however, considerable scatter is also apparent.

The occasional bimodal data distributions among storms and the narrow range of peak flows sampled (figs. 3, 4, and 5) indicate that the autosampler-derived data may be inadequate to develop robust regression models between field parameters and laboratory sample results for Fanno Creek near Durham. Patterns in the autosampler-derived data, however, also support the possibility that such models might be constructed with a more comprehensive dataset. The main limitations of the autosampler data, beyond any serial correlation issues, are that they do not represent all seasons or the high flow conditions, and that some constituent data are bimodal. The incorporation of USGS-NWIS and Clean Water Services ambient monitoring datasets into Scenario 2 and 3 datasets for Fanno Creek, in addition to the autosampler data, was an attempt to overcome these limitations (table 6). Outliers observed in the scatter plots were removed to prevent unacceptable leverage on the regression computations.

Total Suspended Solids

Several regression models for TSS at Fanno Creek near Durham are listed and characterized in table 10. The preferred models produced with each scenario included turbidity and specific conductance as explanatory variables. Discharge (or stage, as a surrogate for discharge) was included as an explanatory variable for Scenarios 1 and 2, but added little information in Model 5, as compared to Model 4, in Scenario 3. The values of the model coefficients for turbidity (0.01 and 0.009) and specific conductance (-0.003 and -0.003) did not change much in Scenario 3, whether or not discharge (Q) was included, nor was there any substantive change in the BCF or adjusted-R^2. Sine and cosine terms were not significant ($p > 0.05$) for the models, indicating that seasonality was either unimportant or was already captured by the continuously monitored variables; these terms are therefore not shown in table 10.

Log transformation of the dependent variable was especially helpful for producing estimated TSS concentrations using continuous monitor data, despite requiring the use of a BCF when transforming the estimated values into normal, non-logarithmic space. In Scenario 1, the coefficients of determination for log-transformed (Model 1, adjusted $R^2 = 0.936$) and non-transformed (Model 2, adjusted $R^2 = 0.956$) TSS are good. However, many non-transformed values of TSS predicted from continuous monitor data using Model 2 (not shown) were negative, particularly outside of the specific calibration period of the autosampler storms; negative predicted TSS values are an unacceptable outcome and render Model 2 unusable. In subsequent regression calculations, the log-transformed values of TSS were always used for the dependent variable.

The use of different data scenarios for developing regression models met with mixed success but illustrates the need for more comprehensive input data. As expected, Scenario 1, using only the autosampler data, produced regressions with high adjusted-R^2 (> 0.90), most likely a result of serial correlation in the autosampler-only data and a small range of environmental conditions sampled; however, the Scenario 1 regressions also had relatively large mean error and validation RMSE values, and non-randomly signed residuals from the sign test, when compared with the broader validation dataset. Model 3 (Scenario 2), combining autosampler data with USGS-NWIS historical data, had similar calibration statistics to Model 6 (Scenario 3) but still may have been affected by serial correlation in the autosampler data. Nonetheless, from the validation process for Model 3, the mean error was intermediate (although indicating a high bias rather than a low bias) and the z-statistic

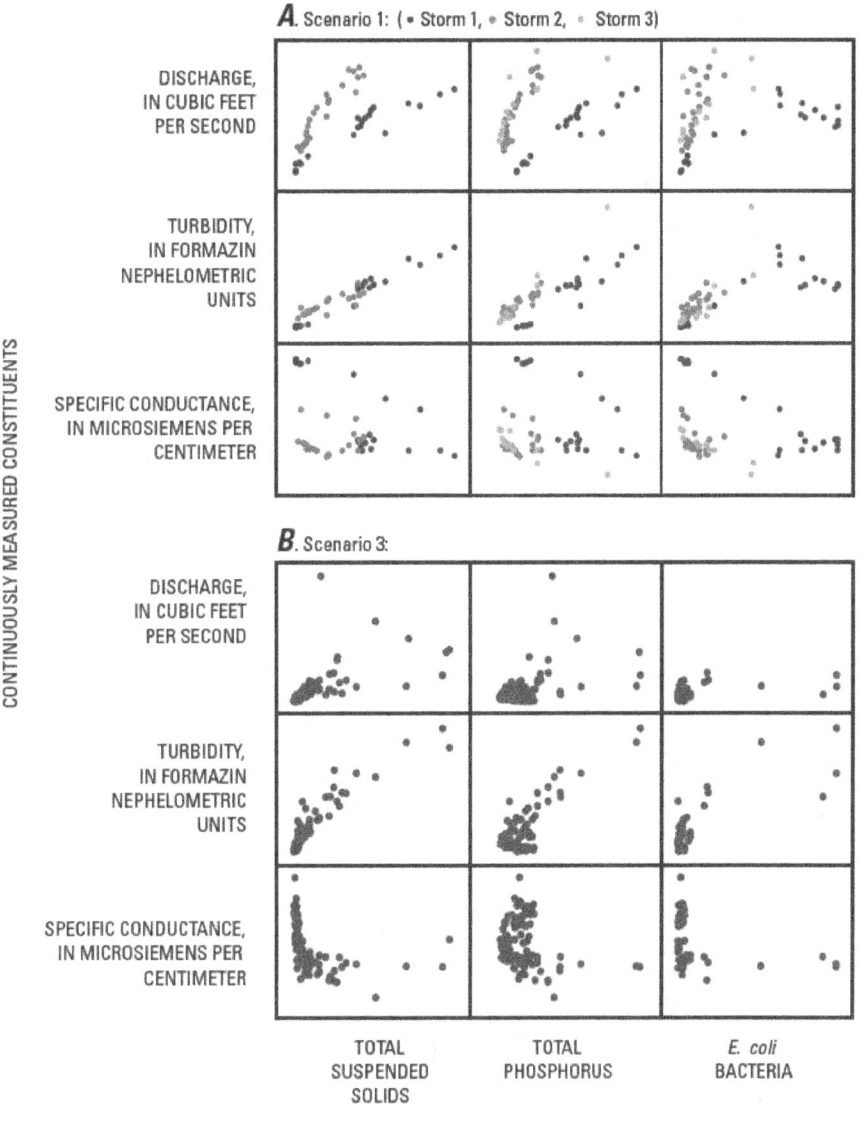

Figure 5. Matrixes of scatter plots of calibration data using (*A*) Scenario 1 and (*B*) Scenario 3 datasets, from Fanno Creek near Durham, Oregon. Scenario 1 data were from autosampler deployments: storm 1, June 17–18, 2002; storm 2, May 4–5, 2003; storm 3, May 8–9, 2003. Data sources for Scenario 3 include U.S. Geological Survey (USGS) historical data, Clean Water Services ambient monitoring, and autosamplers, from 2001 to 2007. All *Escherichia coli* (*E. coli*) bacteria data in (*B*) are from the Clean Water Services ambient monitoring program because no *E. coli* bacteria data were collected by USGS. Units for total suspended solids and total phosphorus are in milligrams per liter, and units for *E. coli* bacteria are in colonies per 100 millimeters.

Table 10. Preliminary model statistics for correlation of total suspended solids with continuous parameters at Fanno Creek near Durham, Oregon.

[Regression models are of the form $TSS = a*Turb + b*Q + c*SC + d$, where a, b, and c are model coefficients and d is the intercept; $Turb$, Q, and SC are the explanatory variables turbidity (in Formazin Nephelometric Units), discharge (in cubic feet per second), and specific conductance (in microsiemens per centimeter), respectively, and TSS is the dependent variable, total suspended solids, in milligrams per liter. In some models, as indicated by the model form column, the dependent or explanatory variables were log transformed. In some models Stage (stream stage, in feet) was used instead of Q, and its coefficient is shown in the 'b' column. Where TSS is log transformed, a bias transformation factor (BCF; Duan, 1983) is multiplied by $10^{(\log TSS)}$ to get the final value. RMSE values are in milligrams per liter. The maximum Variance Inflation Factor (VIF) indicates the largest VIF obtained for any one variable in the correlation. **Abbreviations:** n, number of samples; Adj.-R^2, adjusted R^2, a coefficient of determination, which adjusts for degrees of freedom and penalizes the use of too many explanatory variables; f, a function of indicated constituents; log, base 10 logarithm; RMSE, root mean square error; USGS, U.S. Geological Survey; —, not included in the regression]

Model No. and form	Value of coefficient, when used					Correlation statistics			Model validation—Goodness-of-fit evaluation				
	a	b	c	d	BCF	n	Adj.-R^2	Maximum VIF	Mean error	Validation RMSE	Coefficient of determination	Nash-Sutcliffe coefficient	z-statistic from sign test
Scenario 1	Calibration data set—Autosamplers only								Validation data set—Clean Water Services ambient monitoring data				
1. logTSS=f(logTurb, logStage, logSC)	1.19	2.56	2.1	-6.09	1.03	54	0.936	2.8	-1.9	12.9	0.83	0.78	5.35
2. TSS=f(Turb, logStage, logSC)	1.32	132.1	156.6	-414.6	—	54	0.956	2.4	-8.5	168	0.71	0.58	5.95
Scenario 2	Calibration data set—Complete autosampler storm samples + USGS 2001–07								Validation data set—Clean Water Services ambient monitoring data				
3. logTSS=f(Turb, logQ, logSC)	0.011	0.432	0.49	-0.834	1.1	131	0.848	[1]4.1	4.1	38.6	0.83	-0.94	1.51
Scenario 3	Calibration data set—Peak autosampler plus first monthly and high flow monitoring samples from USGS and Clean Water Services datasets								Validation data set—Remaining monthly low flow USGS + Clean Water Services ambient monitoring + non-peak autosampler data				
4. logTSS=f(Turb, SC)	0.01	—	-0.003	1.42	1.06	96	0.885	1.7	-0.58	8.44	0.04	0.02	1.67
5. logTSS=f(Turb, Q, SC)	0.01	0.0006	-0.003	1.35	1.05	96	0.885	2.2	-0.52	8.42	0.04	0.03	2.12
6. logTSS=f(Turb, logQ, logSC)	0.009	0.224	-0.5	1.69	1.04	96	0.897	4.4	-0.85	30.8	0.05	0.04	1

[1] Exceeds a threshold VIF value, calculated as $\{1/(1-(Adj.-R^2)\}$ and indicates possible multicollinearity.

from the sign test was considerably lower than the models from Scenario 1; also, the coefficient of determination (0.83) was the among the highest of all models. Despite the more randomly signed residuals, the Nash-Sutcliffe coefficient for Scenario 2 indicates that the predictive power of Model 3 may be worse than using the mean of the laboratory data. For Scenario 3 (which uses high-flow data from USGS and Clean Water Services, with monthly Clean Water Services ambient monitoring data and the peak discharge samples from the autosampler deployment), the regression coefficients, correlation statistics, and validation statistics were similar with or without discharge (Models 4 and 5). Model 6 was evaluated to test the importance of log transformation of the explanatory variables in Scenario 3, but this transformation increased the mean error and RMSE for the validation statistics. All Scenario 3 models had poor coefficients of determination (<0.1) and Nash-Sutcliffe coefficients (<0.1), suggesting that they did not reproduce the validation data well, and that the means of the validation data would provide estimates that were as good or better than the model estimates. However, because the validation data are heavily weighted towards base-flow conditions, and the objective of the modeling exercise is primarily to predict the high constituent concentrations during stormflows, these coefficients probably do not adequately reflect the utility of the model.

Model 5 produced diagnostic statistics equivalent to Model 4 but used an extra variable, discharge (Q), indicating that Model 5 probably is overfitted and therefore less robust (Helsel and Hirsch, 1992), and that Model 4 may be the most appropriate functional form given the available datasets. Conversely, specific conductance has little physical relevance to TSS other than as a surrogate for discharge, yet it was an important variable in all models. VIF values were less than 5 for all independent variables in the models shown; however, the largest VIF for Model 3 (for log$Q$) exceeded the VIF$_{crit}$. Log$Q$ was highly significant in the model (p <0.0001, not shown); whereas logSC was only slightly significant (p = 0.07). The inclusion of discharge as an independent variable may be needed to represent mid-winter, high-flow conditions. Specific conductance was a significant (p<0.05) model coefficient in all other models. The relatively low VIF$_{crit}$ for Model 3 may be a reflection of the Scenario 2 dataset and the model's relatively low adjusted-R^2.

Plotting a time series of the measured TSS concentrations against those predicted using the regression models allows the overall results of the model to be evaluated qualitatively. Individual data from the Scenario 3 calibration and validation datasets and the results from spring 2002 until summer 2003 including the 95 percent prediction interval of Model 4, are shown in figure 6. This period includes the two storms when the autosampler was deployed (table 9), and encompasses January 2003 when the station was moved from Durham City Park to Durham Road (fig. 6). Upon a cursory inspection, the model seems to predict slightly lower baseline TSS concentrations prior to moving the station. However, this period also predominantly encompasses spring–autumn, 2002, with naturally lower discharges; whereas the period after January 2003 is predominantly winter, characterized by higher discharges, so it is reasonable to expect higher baseline TSS concentrations in the winter. Calibration and verification data, which (except for the autosampler data) were collected at the Durham Road site, also show this shift, indicating that moving the station had a negligible effect on model calibration and predictions.

Although Scenario 3 demonstrates the type of dataset that may be most appropriate for developing robust regression models (that is, data that are independent, year-round, and include high-flow samples), validation of results from Models 4, 5, and 6 is hampered because few high-flow samples are included in either the calibration or validation datasets. Many high TSS concentrations are predicted but few calibration or validation data points are present during the high TSS events for comparison (fig. 6). Model 4 appears to be the most robust model for TSS at Fanno Creek, on the basis of up-front assumptions about the value of the different potential calibration datasets, and on the results in table 10 (the relatively low coefficient of determination [0.04] from the validation dataset notwithstanding). Visually, figure 6 shows that the storm-related predictions are relatively accurate for the moderate-sized storms represented in the available datasets. The log-scale used on the y-axis in figure 6 can cause a misperception in the magnitude of errors: during base-flow conditions, the model appears to slightly overpredict TSS concentrations; however, the actual errors are small compared to those at higher concentrations. Validation of these models at higher concentrations cannot be accomplished with the available data.

Comparing the measured and predicted values directly provides additional perspective into the uncertainties and limitations of the available datasets and models (fig. 7). That comparison, using results from Model 4, shows that the indicated prediction interval spans a range of almost an order of magnitude (~0.75 log units) for a given measured value. Available measured-TSS data are relatively well represented up to about 10^2 (or 100) mg/L, with a few additional samples at slightly higher concentrations up to about $10^{2.5}$ (or 316) mg/L.

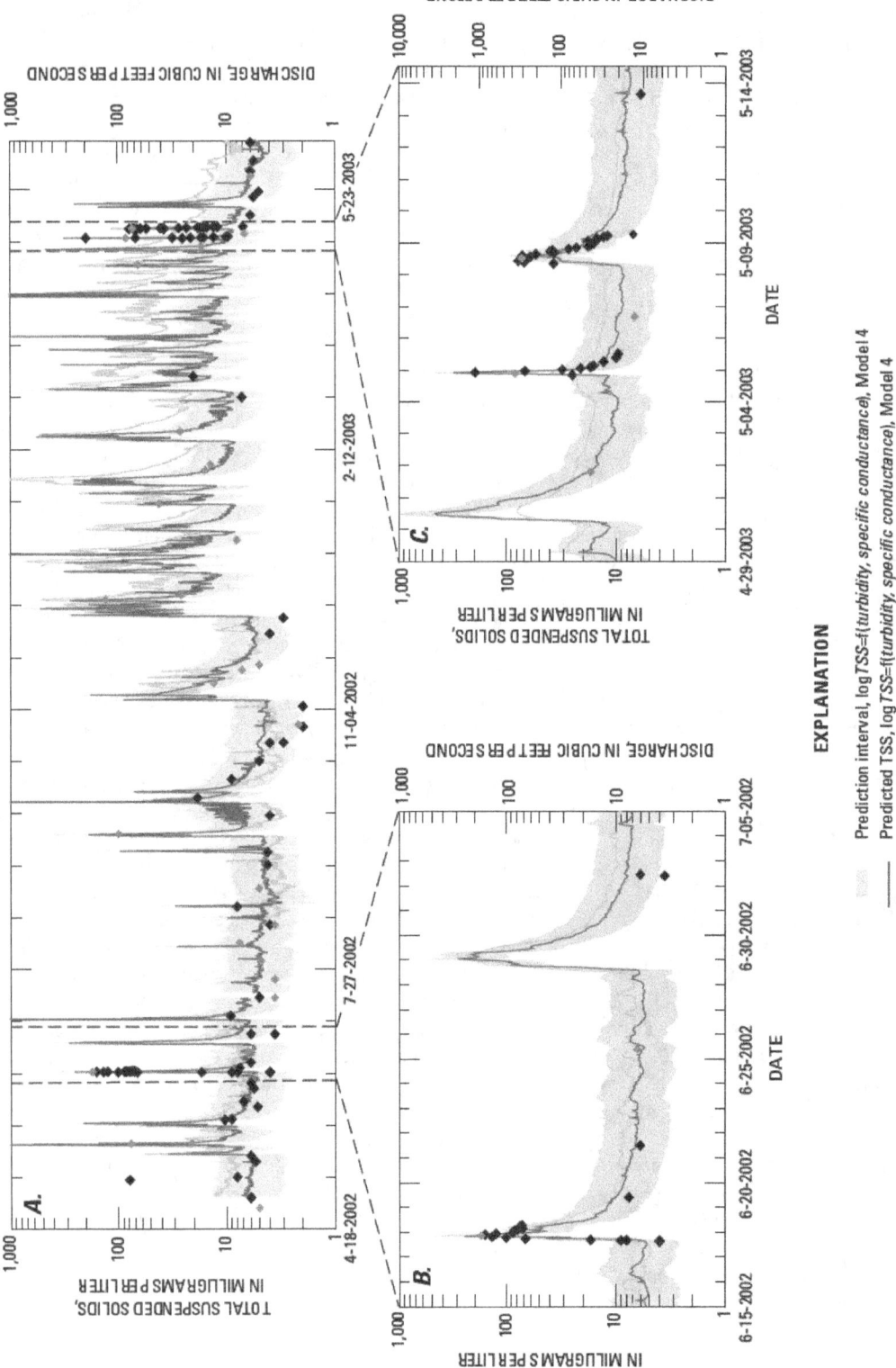

EXPLANATION

Prediction interval, logTSS=f(turbidity, specific conductance), Model 4

Predicted TSS, logTSS=f(turbidity, specific conductance), Model 4

Discharge

Validation data, Scenario 3

Calibration data, Scenario 3

Figure 6. Time series of predicted concentrations of total suspended solids (TSS) at Fanno Creek for Model 4, with prediction intervals and calibration and validation data (A) during 2002–03, (B) during storm 1, and (C) during storms 2 and 3, Tualatin River basin, Oregon. Discharge is shown to indicate timing of events.

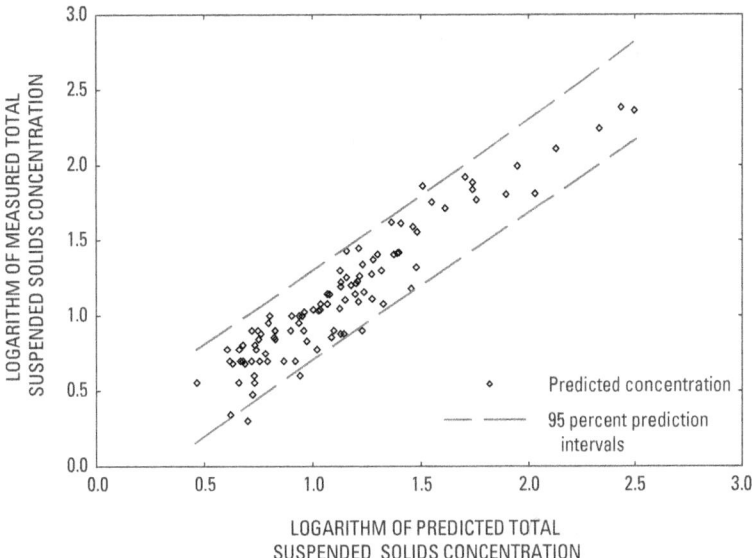

Figure 7. Comparison of concentrations of measured and predicted total suspended solids from Model 4, using the calibration dataset from Scenario 3, Fanno Creek near Durham, Oregon. Native reporting units for total suspended solids concentrations prior to log transformation were in milligrams per liter.

Total Phosphorus

Example regression models for TP at the Fanno Creek site are shown in table 11. As for TSS, initial results for TP produced many negative predictions when TP was not log transformed (Scenario 1, Model 3), despite the adjusted-R^2 being relatively high (0.905). Bias correction factors for all models with log-transformation of TP (that is, all except Model 3) were similar, ranging from 1.01 to 1.03. Log transformation of explanatory variables was evaluated in Model 2 and does not seem to provide any benefit. The resulting adjusted-R^2 is slightly lower than for non-transformation of the same variables (Model 1), and the regression RMSE is slightly larger. Validation statistics for Model 2 also are poorer than for Model 1. Sine and cosine terms were not significant, indicating that no seasonal cycles were present that were not already expressed by the other independent variables.

Adjusted-R^2 values for Scenario 1 (calibration using autosampler data only) generally were higher than for Scenarios 2 and 3, which may be an artifact of serial correlation in the autosampler data, and fewer data representing the range of variability from different seasons or more high-flow events. Although turbidity seems to be the most directly linear predictor of TP when examined graphically from the autosampler data alone (fig. 5), specific conductance also was repeatedly an important independent variable in the regression process (table 11).

Table 11. Preliminary model statistics for correlation of total phosphorus with continuous parameters at Fanno Creek near Durham, Oregon.

[Regression models are of the form $TP = a*Turb + b*Q + c*SC + d$, where a, b, and c are regression coefficients and d is the intercept, $Turb$, Q, and SC are the explanatory variables turbidity (in Formazin Nephelometric Units), discharge (in cubic feet per second), and specific conductance (in microsiemens per centimeter), respectively, and TP is the dependent variable, total phosphorus concentration, in milligrams per liter. In some models, as indicated by the model form column, the dependent or explanatory variables were log transformed. Where TP is log transformed, a bias transformation factor (BCF; Duan, 1983) is multiplied by $10^{(\log TP)}$ to get the final value. RMSE values are in milligrams per liter. The maximum Variance Inflation Factor (VIF) indicates the largest VIF obtained for any one variable in the correlation. **Abbreviations:** n, number of samples; Adj.-R^2, adjusted R^2, a coefficient of determination, which adjusts for degrees of freedom and penalizes the use of too many explanatory variables; f, a function of indicated constituents; log, base 10 logarithm; RMSE, root mean square error; USGS, U.S. Geological Survey; —, not included in the regression]

Model No. and form	Model calibration								Model validation – Goodness-of-fit evaluation				
	Value of coefficient, when used					Correlation statistics			Mean error	Validation RMSE	Coefficient of determination	Nash-Sutcliffe coefficient	z-statistic from sign test
	a	b	c	d	BCF	n	Adj.-R^2	Maximum VIF					
Scenario 1	**Calibration data set**— Autosamplers only								**Validation data set**— Clean Water Services ambient monitoring data				
1. $\log TP$=f($Turb$, SC)	0.007	—	0.003	-1.63	1.01	54	0.893	1.3	-0.003	0.075	0.24	-0.1	1.1
2. $\log TP$=f($\log Turb$, $\log SC$)	0.752	—	2.05	-6.47	1.02	54	0.813	1.7	-0.039	0.092	0.05	-0.67	5.2
3. TP=f($Turb$, SC)	0.004	—	0.001	-0.2	—	54	0.905	1.3	-0.007	0.072	0.20	-0.01	1.3
Scenario 2	**Calibration data set**— Complete autosampler storm samples + USGS 2001–07								**Validation data set**— Clean Water Services ambient monitoring data				
4. $\log TP$=f($Turb$, SC)	0.006	—	0.002	-1.34	1.03	140	0.645	1.7	-0.008	0.064	0.29	0.19	1.7
Scenario 3	**Calibration data set**— Peak autosampler plus first monthly and high flow monitoring samples from USGS and Clean Water Services datasets								**Validation data set**—remaining monthly low flow USGS + Clean Water Services ambient monitoring + non-peak autosampler data				
5. $\log TP$=f($Turb$, SC)	0.005	—	0.001	-1.19	1.02	99	0.575	[1]1.6	-0.02	0.067	<0.01	-0.14	3.1
6. $\log TP$=f($Turb$, Q, SC)	0.005	-0.00003	0.001	-1.18	1.02	95	0.582	[1]2.0	-0.021	0.067	<0.01	-0.16	4

[1] Exceeds a critical threshold VIF value (VIF_{crit}), calculated as $\{1/(1–(Adj.-R^2)\}$ and indicates possible multicollinearity.

Discharge, which often is significantly correlated with turbidity and TSS as well as TP, was evaluated for Fanno Creek in the scenario using high-flow data (Scenario 3, Model 6). Model results using discharge were not noticeably better than those in Model 5 without it, and its inclusion in models would likely result in overfitting. Although Model 5 is presumed, like Model 4 for TSS, the most robust because the input dataset is the most comprehensive and the least affected by serial correlation, the model's correlation and validation statistics were relatively poor. In particular, the coefficients of determination for the initial model calibration (adjusted-R^2 = 0.575) and for the validation (<0.01) indicate substantial room for improvement, although the validation dataset may not have a large enough range in TP to be useful for an R^2 determination. Turbidity and specific conductance in Model 5 have VIF values exceeding the VIF_{crit}, but both variables are highly significant in the model (p <0.0001) indicating that the VIF_{crit} which is low because of the low adjusted-R^2, does not accurately reflect the severity of multicollinearity. In Model 6, discharge is not a significant variable (p = 0.89, not shown) and seems to contribute to multicollinearity problems.

The predicted results from Model 5 were biased low compared to the validation dataset in Scenario 3, which could be a result of the large amount of calibration data representing baseline rather than high-flow conditions. These goodness-of-fit statistics, like those for TSS at the Fanno Creek site, are a measure primarily of the base flow rather than high-flow conditions, due to a relative lack of high-flow data for comparison. The model, therefore, is not necessarily as poor as the goodness-of-fit statistics might indicate, and the model predictions during storms probably still have some value.

Models 1, 4, and 5 are of the form logTP = f ($Turb$, SC), using datasets from Scenarios 1, 2, and 3, and their respective model coefficients and BCFs are relatively similar (table 11). The same is true of their model validation statistics; although the coefficient of determination and the Nash-Sutcliffe coefficient are the best for Model 4, no model's validation statistics are particularly good. Although the VIFs indicate possible multicollinearity in Model 5, this is a result of the model's adjusted-R^2 being relatively low. It is, therefore, reasonable that this model form is appropriate for TP at Fanno Creek near Durham, but that gathering larger, more applicable

datasets with high-flow samples will result in more refined model coefficients (the values for a, c, d, and BCF in table 11) rather than changing the functional form of the model.

Despite the relatively poor correlation and validation statistics mentioned above, the predicted results from Model 5 appear to capture the overall pattern of TP concentrations in Fanno Creek reasonably well (fig. 8), especially at low flow conditions. Most observed values are well within the 95 percent prediction interval for the model, despite often being separated from the model's prediction line. A few high spikes in concentration are predicted during winter events (fig. 8A) when concentrations may reach 10 mg/L or higher; however, the accuracy of these spikes cannot be evaluated because no samples representing those events were available. The model also achieved a reasonable representation of TP during storms when the autosamplers were in use, June 2002 and May 2003.

Baseline conditions in the data are well represented in the model, with relatively constant average concentrations about 0.1–0.15 mg/L. Observed concentrations during summer 2002 were slightly higher than the predicted values, whereas in Winter 2002–03 they were slightly lower than those predicted, but the differences are within the uncertainty range indicated by the prediction interval. These differences are unrelated to the relocation of the continuous monitor from Durham City Park (site 1a in fig. 2) to Durham Road (site 1b in fig. 2), because that relocation would only affect the predicted concentrations rather than the observed. Instead, with generally higher discharges during winter samplings, the TP concentrations may be diluted during certain conditions such as the falling limb of storm hydrographs as reported by Anderson and Rounds (2003). With the exception of the autosampler data, most data in the Scenario 3 calibration and validation datasets were collected without regard to storm conditions and many were collected immediately after storm discharge peaks. Discharge is not included as an independent variable in Model 5, and generally was not significant in the candidate models (table 11). Future formulations of a model for TP at Fanno Creek may be enhanced by evaluating a model calibrated specifically for winter periods.

A comparison of measured and predicted TP concentrations illustrates that most of the available data occupy a relatively narrow range of TP concentrations, from about $10^{-1.2}$ to $10^{-0.8}$ (or about 0.06 to 0.16) mg/L, with only a few at higher concentrations being represented (fig. 9).

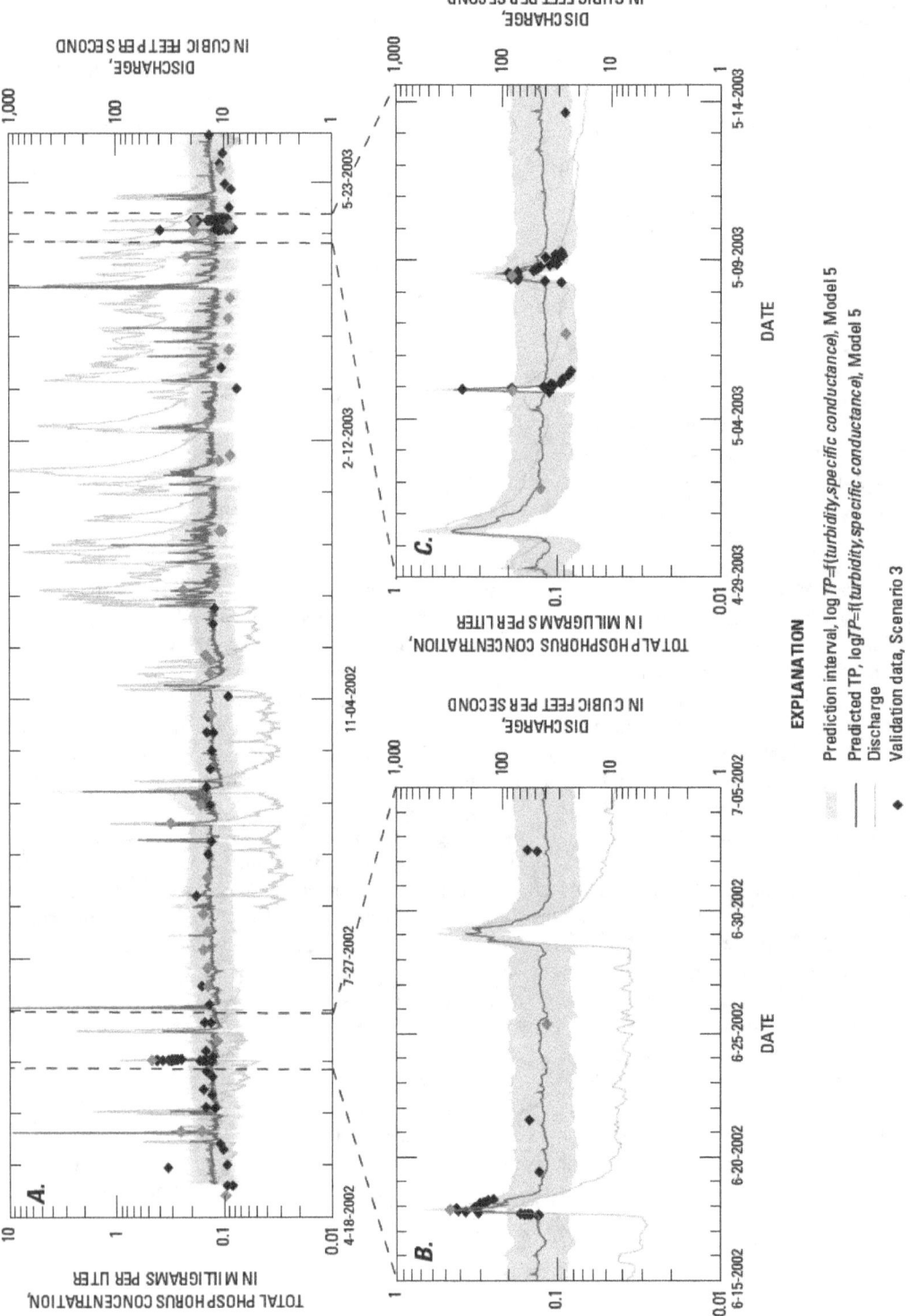

Figure 8.   Time series of predicted total phosphorus (TP) concentrations at Fanno Creek from Model 5, with prediction intervals, calibration, and validation data (*A*) during 2002–03, (*B*) during storm 1, and (*C*) during storms 2 and 3, Tualatin River basin, Oregon. Discharge is shown to indicate timing of events.

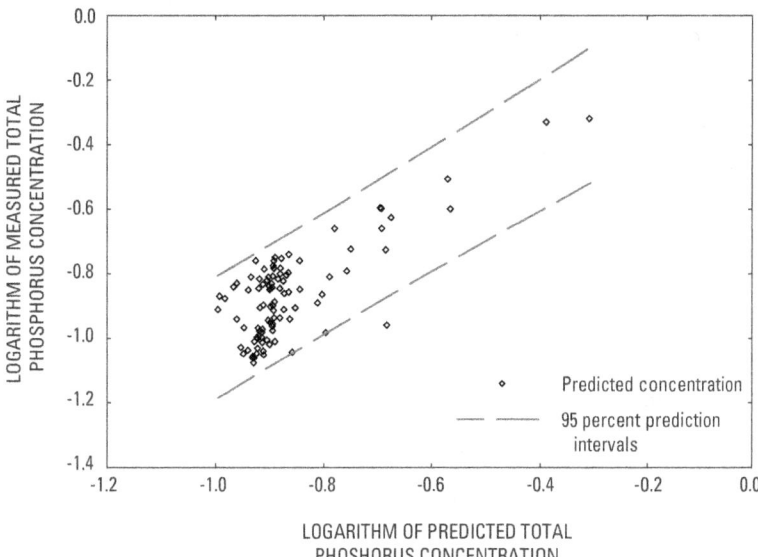

Figure 9. Comparison of concentrations of measured and predicted total phosphorus from Model 5, using the calibration dataset from Scenario 3, Fanno Creek near Durham, Oregon. Native reporting units for total phosphorus concentrations prior to log transformation were in milligrams per liter.

Escherichia coli Bacteria

Model results for *E. coli* bacteria were moderately successful (table 12), with several model forms having similar coefficients and reasonably strong adjusted-R^2 values (0.586–0.713). No data on *E. coli* bacteria were available from the USGS databases, so the data for calibration were available for Scenarios 1 and 3 only, modified by the lack of USGS data. Models 1–5 used log-transformation of *E. coli* bacteria counts, and each model used turbidity as an explanatory variable. In Models 1, 3, 4, and 5, in which turbidity is not transformed, the regression coefficients for turbidity (0.014–0.016) and the intercepts (2.17–2.53) vary only slightly. The addition of discharge as an explanatory variable, whether or not it was transformed, was not particularly useful, as evidenced by the lack of changes in the coefficients for turbidity, minor increases in the models' adjusted-R^2, and substantial increases in validation RMSE when discharge was added. Bias correction factors were all relatively large, particularly for the Scenario 3 datasets (about 1.4–1.5), indicating substantial negative bias in the uncorrected values. Once again, sine and cosine terms were not significant, so no models using them are shown. Goodness-of-fit statistics indicate relatively large uncertainty in the predicted values compared to the validation data, with a large (negative) mean error and RMSE values measured that mostly are about 1,000 or more for the Scenario 3 dataset. Model 6 had the highest adjusted-R^2 for calibration in Scenario 3, and the coefficient of determination and Nash-Sutcliffe coefficient were high (0.69 and 0.69, respectively). However, the explanatory and dependent variables were untransformed, and many predicted values during the modeled 2002–03 time period were negative, rendering Model 6 unusable for general purposes. Regression coefficients for the independent variables and intercept in Model 6 were 2–3 orders of magnitude higher than those in the other models, which is an artifact of the lack of log transformation.

All models with more than one independent variable were possibly affected by multicollinearity, despite maximum VIF values that were less than 3, again reflecting the relatively low adjusted-R^2 values for the models. In each case, the statistical significance of the discharge term was poor (p = 0.003, 0.438, 0.233, and 0.0025 for Models 2, 4, 5, and 6, respectively). Thus, the addition of discharge increased multicollinearity without an offsetting gain in model confidence.

Given the results from table 12, with previous assumptions that Scenario 3 represents the most appropriate input data available, Model 3 then represents the presumed best available model for *E. coli* bacteria. Predicted data from Model 3, together with the 95 percent prediction interval and the calibration and validation datasets are shown in figure 10. The prediction interval is substantially larger for models predicting *E. coli* bacteria than for TSS or TP, spanning almost 2 orders of magnitude. The model predicts baseline *E. coli* bacteria counts of about 300 colonies/100 mL during summer 2002, which is close to the single-sample water quality standard of 406 colonies/100 mL. It also predicts closer to 400–500 colonies/100 mL during Winter 2003, overpredicting most calibration and validation samples and indicating

that baseline predictions may have little utility. The model predicts numerous peaks of 10,000–100,000 colonies/100 mL, and mirrors the pattern of turbidity and discharge in Fanno Creek. Because most Clean Water Services monitoring data are from relatively low-flow conditions, few data are available to confirm these high counts, although the model accounts reasonably well for the variability observed over the hydrographs during storms sampled by the autosamplers in June 2002 and May 2003 (fig. 10*B* and *C*). Quantitation of *E. coli* bacteria at concentrations greater than about 1,000 colonies/100 mL is not routinely done by the Clean Water Services laboratory owing to the difficulty of differentiating tightly packed colonies grown on agar, or the nonconservative nature of large dilutions for bacterial growth (J. Miller, Clean Water Services, oral commun., June 2008). For that reason, obtaining reliable data from storms to calibrate or validate these or subsequent *E. coli* bacteria models may be difficult.

Prediction intervals for *E. coli* bacteria from Model 3 range almost 2 orders of magnitude (fig. 11). Measured data (that is, samples) are predominantly at low *E. coli* bacteria counts, with only a few from counts greater than 10^3 (1,000) colonies/100 mL. The model captures some trends in the measured bacteria concentrations, showing that the explanatory variable (turbidity) has some predictive information, but the uncertainty is large enough that this particular model has limited application until a better dataset becomes available. On the other hand, if use of the model were limited to predicting periods when bacterial counts exceed a threshold value such as 1,000 colonies/100 mL, rather than quantifying the actual peak values, model 3 might be adequate.

Table 12. Preliminary model statistics for correlation of *Escherichia coli* bacteria with continuous parameters at Fanno Creek near Durham, Oregon.

[No Scenario 2 data sets were available because USGS did not collect *E. coli* data during the study period. Regression models are of the form $E. coli = a*Turb + b*Q + c*SC + d$, where a, b, and c are regression coefficients and d is the intercept, *Turb*, *Q*, and *SC* are the explanatory variables turbidity (in Formazin Nephelometric Units), discharge (in cubic feet per second), and specific conductance (in microsiemens per centimeter), respectively, and *E. coli* is the dependent variable, *E. coli* bacteria counts, in colonies per 100 milliliters. In some models, as indicated by the model form column, the dependent or explanatory variables were log transformed. Where *E. coli* is log transformed, a bias transformation factor (BCF; Duan, 1983) is multiplied by $10^{\log E. coli}$ to get the final value. RMSE values are in colonies per 100 mL. The maximum Variance Inflation Factor (VIF) indicates the largest VIF obtained for any one variable in the correlation. **Abbreviations:** *n*, number of samples; Adj.-R^2, adjusted R^2, a coefficient of determination which adjusts for degrees of freedom and penalizes the use of too many explanatory variables; f, a function of indicated constituents; *E. coli*, *Escherichia coli* bacteria; log, base 10 logarithm; RMSE, root mean square error; USGS, U.S. Geological Survey; –, not included in the regression]

Model No. and form	Model calibration					Correlation statistics			Model validation – Goodness-of-fit evaluation				
	Value of coefficient, when used					*n*	Adj.-R^2	Maximum VIF	Mean error	Validation RMSE	Coefficient of determination	Nash-Sutcliffe coefficient	z-statistic from sign test
	a	b	c	d	BCF								
Scenario 1	Calibration data set—Autosamplers only								Validation data set—Clean Water Services ambient monitoring data				
1. log*E. coli*=f(*Turb*)	0.014	–	–	2.53	1.22	54	0.692	–	528.3	196.6	0.50	-2.2	5.45
2. log*E. coli*=f(log*Turb*, log*Q*)	1.69	-0.702	–	1.76	1.19	54	0.713	[1]2.7	219.2	1.760	0.36	0.25	2.09
Scenario 3	Calibration data set—Peak autosampler plus first monthly and high flow monitoring samples from Clean Water Services dataset								Validation data set—Remaining monthly low flow Clean Water Services ambient monitoring + non-peak autosampler data				
3. log*E. coli*=f(*Turb*)	0.014	–	–	2.17	1.53	40	0.590	–	-454	996	0.31	0.16	1.86
4. log*E. coli*=f(*Turb*, *Q*)	0.016	-0.002	–	2.21	1.42	40	0.586	[1]2.6	-407	2,470	0.31	0.07	2.06
5. log*E. coli*=f(*Turb*, log*Q*)	0.016	-0.18	–	2.39	1.43	40	0.595	[1]1.7	-410	1,077	0.28	0.004	2.06
6. *E. coli*=f(*Turb*,*Q*)	103.7	-28.4	–	-2.39	–	40	0.7	[1]2.3	-81	1,425	0.69	0.69	1.07

[1]Exceeds a threshold VIF value, calculated as {1/(1−(Adj.-R^2)} and indicates possible multicollinearity.

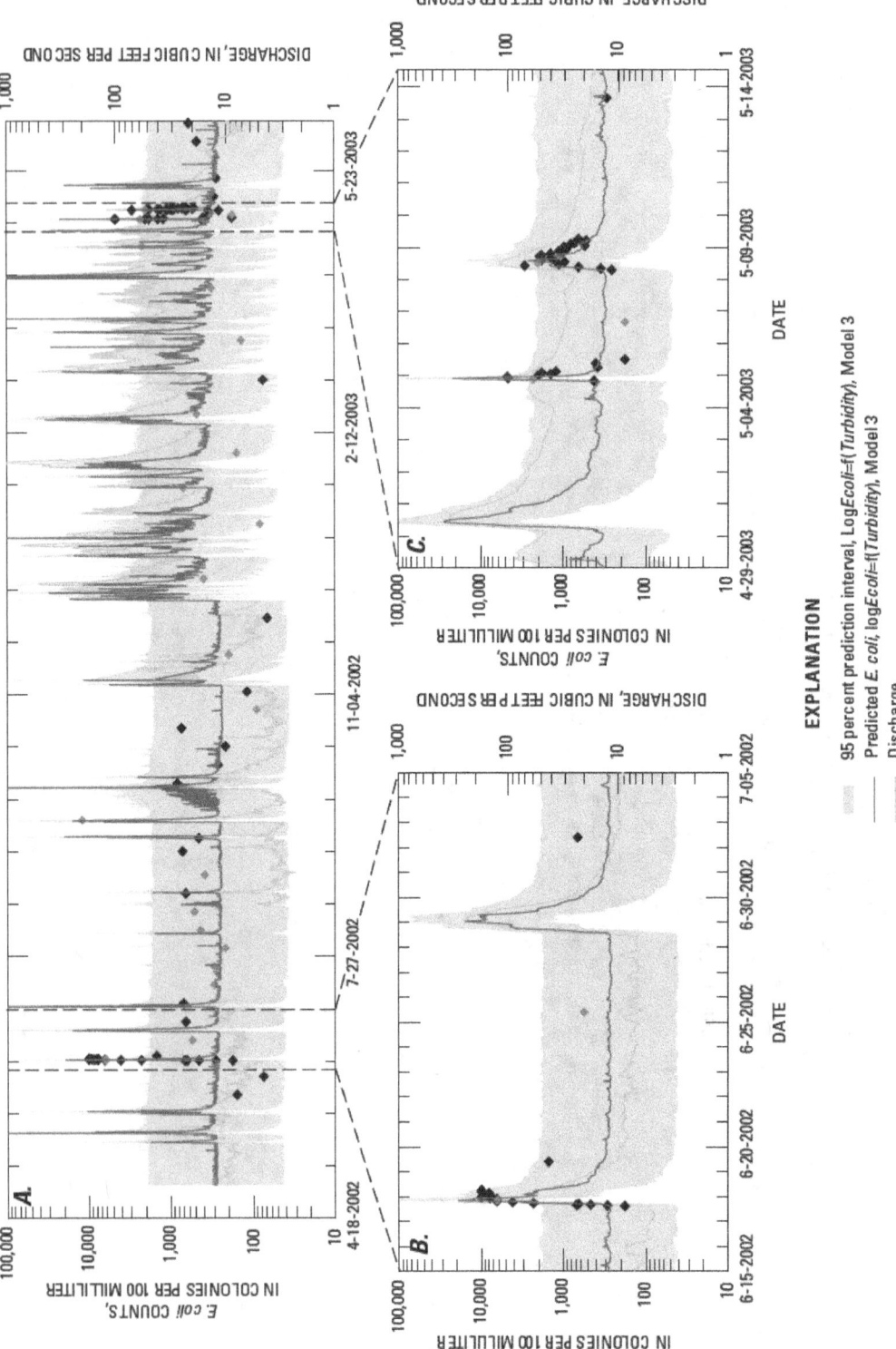

Figure 10. Time series of predicted *Escherichia coli* (*E. coli*) bacteria counts at Fanno Creek from Model 3, with prediction intervals, calibration, and validation data (*A*) during 2002–03, (*B*) during storm 1, and (*C*) during storms 2 and 3, Tualatin River basin, Oregon. Discharge is shown to indicate timing of events.

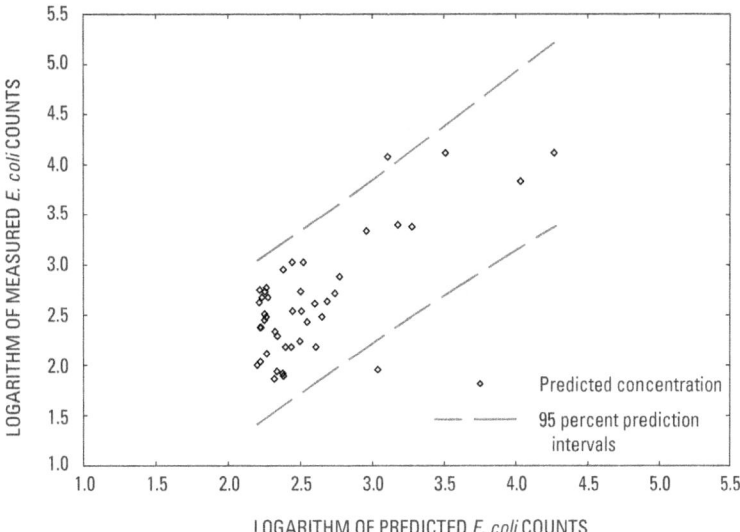

Figure 11. Comparison of concentrations of measured and predicted *Escherichia coli* (*E. coli*) bacteria counts from Model 3, using the calibration dataset from Scenario 3, Fanno Creek near Durham, Oregon. Native reporting units for *Escherichia coli* bacteria counts prior to log transformation were in colonies per 100 milliliters.

Dairy Creek at Highway 8

Autosampler Data

The response of Dairy Creek to storm runoff is different than that of many other streams included in this study. The Dairy Creek basin is predominately agricultural and is relatively insensitive to runoff from small- to medium-sized storms unless antecedent rainfall is high, a characteristic that is likely related to the small amount of impervious land upstream of the sampling site and the relatively low surrounding topographic relief. Prolonged dry conditions during summer cause streamflow to recede and several consecutive days to weeks of rain are usually required for streamflow to increase.

Once the soils are well saturated in autumn, streamflow in Dairy Creek tends to increase rapidly to relatively high levels and remains sustained for long periods during the winter until conditions begin to dry in late spring. Also potentially contributing to the hydrological and chemical response of the drainage basin, about 36 percent of the agricultural land in the Dairy Creek basin uses subsurface drainage or tile drains (U.S. Department of Agriculture, 1995). Tile drains are used where soil drainage is poor, allowing cultivation on lands that might otherwise preclude agricultural activities. However, tile drains also can provide an effective route for preferential flow of water and solutes to streams, speeding hydrologic response and reducing chemical transformations such as uptake, adhesion, or degradation (Stone and Wilson, 2006). The actual effect of tile drains was not evaluated directly in this study.

During the study period, the continuous monitor at Dairy Creek was deployed seasonally. The monitor was installed in spring when stage receded to allow wading, and removed in the autumn when stage was expected to become high. Backwater from the Tualatin River was sometimes the cause of high stages that limited access to the creek. As a result of the winter high stages, neither continuous monitor nor discharge data are available at Dairy Creek during the winter and early spring months (about November–May), limiting the ability to make predictions during those periods. Stream stage, which was the only continuously recorded parameter during the winter months in the study period, can be a useful surrogate for discharge.

Individual storms were sampled during October 2003 by autosamplers at Dairy Creek, with relatively little antecedent rainfall, and November 2003, with slightly wetter antecedent conditions than the October storm. The pattern of events sampled resulted in streamflow and water-quality conditions that were different between storms (although the stage during storms remained less than 10 ft). Therefore, data for discharge, stage, turbidity, and specific conductance had bimodal distributions that were dominated by storm-to-storm differences when all samples were included (fig. 12A). Specific conductance, in particular, showed little variability during the October 2003 storm, and varied only by about 5 percent during the November 2003 storm. In contrast to the autosampler data, the Clean Water Services ambient monitoring dataset includes numerous samples with stages greater than 10 ft (maximum 22.42 ft) during 2002-04.

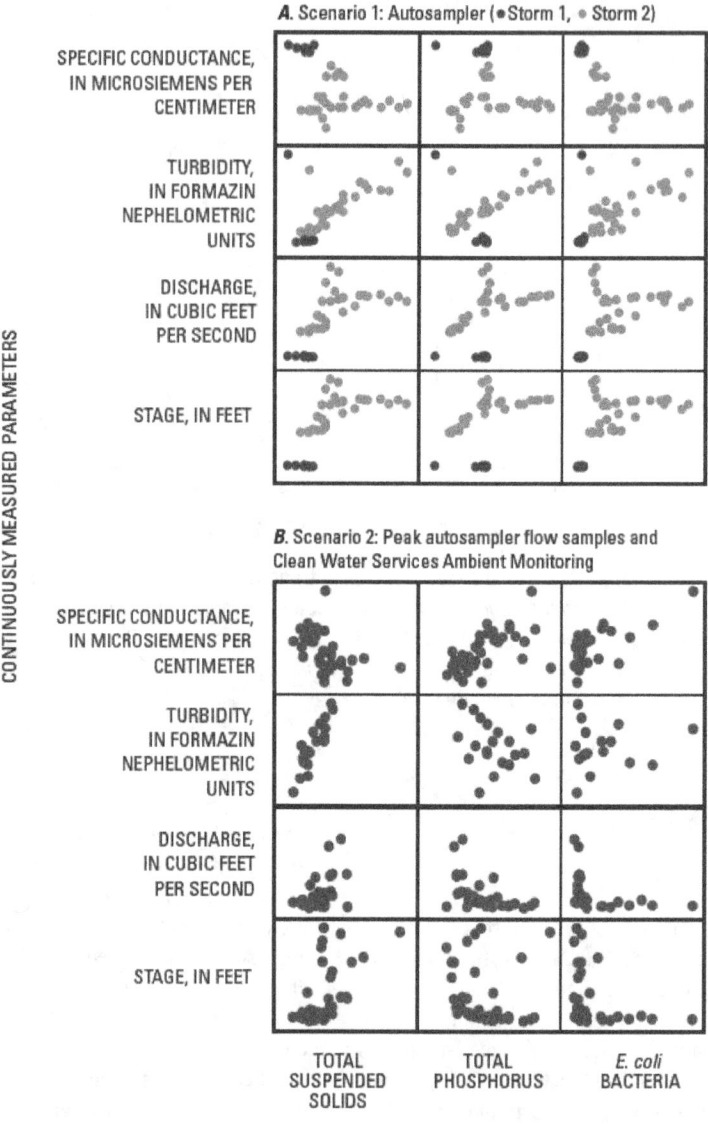

Figure 12.   Matrixes of scatter plots of calibration data from Dairy Creek at Highway 8 near Hillsboro, Oregon, using (*A*) Scenario 1 and (*B*) Scenario 2 datasets. Scenario 1 data were from autosampler deployments: storm 1, October 9, 2003; storm 2, November 19–20, 2003. Data sources for Scenario 2 include Clean Water Services ambient monitoring and autosamplers. Units for total suspended solids and total phosphorus are in milligrams per liter, and units for *Escherichia coli* (*E. coli*) bacteria are in colonies per 100 milliliter.

Linear relationships between turbidity and TSS were evident in both the autosampler-only and larger combined (Scenario 2) datasets; however, few other constituent pairs have apparent linear relations at the Dairy Creek site.

The sampling during storm 1 was triggered by an individual turbidity value (32 FNU) from the continuous monitor that was greater than the autosampler threshold value used to initiate sampling (25 FNU); however, turbidity values were less than 10 FNU in most subsequent samples. A slight increase in stream stage accompanied this storm and the samples were retained for analysis, despite the relatively modest overall storm response. Consequently, the sampler had been removed for cleaning before a larger storm several days later, which may have produced a broader range of values for field parameters and laboratory constituents. Soils

in the drainage basin were apparently well saturated by the November 2003 storm, and stream stage increased to levels that were too high to collect samples.

Specific conductance during autosampler deployments was representative of mostly average conditions, ranging from 117 to 140 µS/cm, values that were exceeded about 40–70 percent of the time during the study period (fig. 13A). The sampled turbidity data represented a broader range of conditions at Dairy Creek, ranging from about 6 to 30 FNU, values that were exceeded between 1 and almost 90 percent of the time during the study period (fig. 13B). Recall, however, that the dataset used to determine these exceedances was derived from monitoring data that did not include winter high-flow conditions.

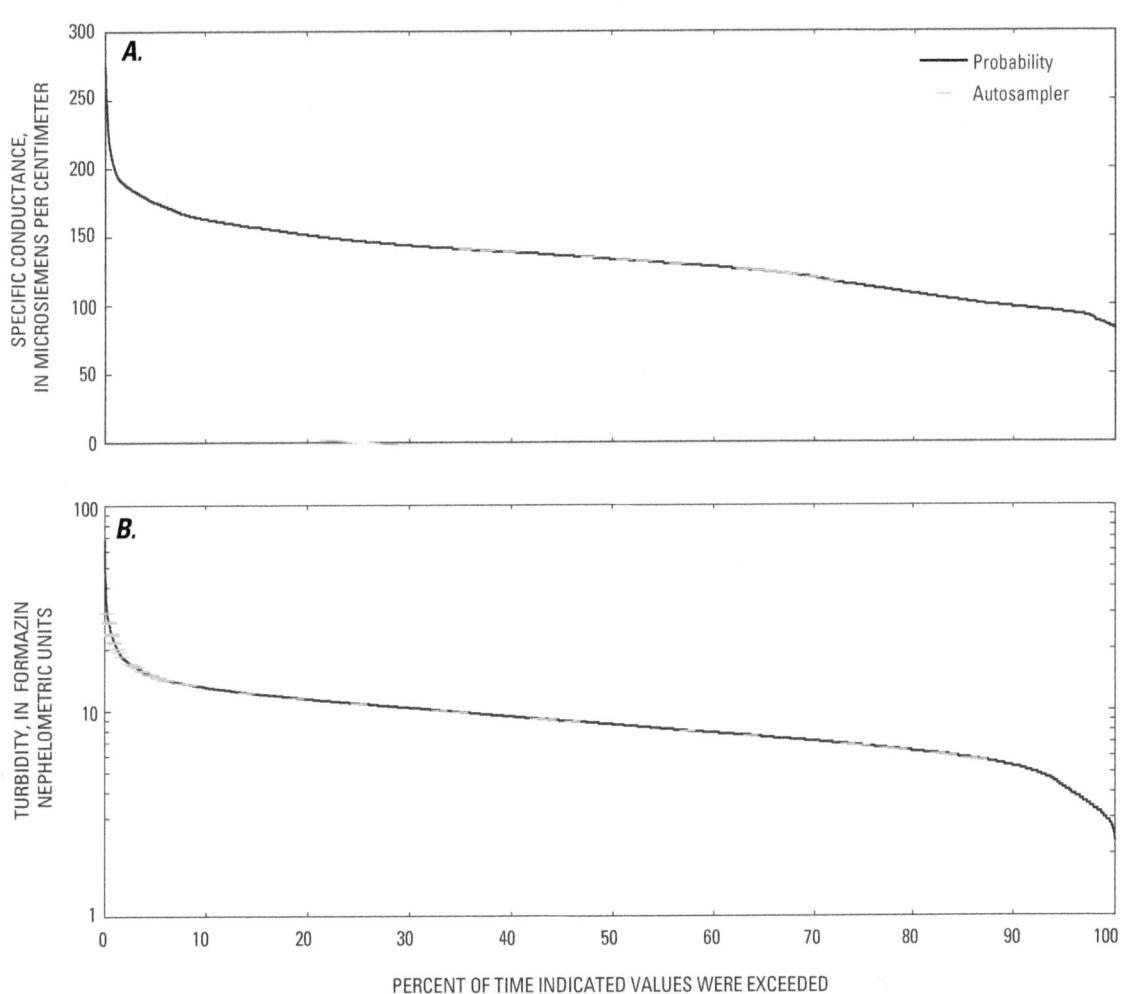

Figure 13.   Probability that (A) specific conductances and (B) turbidities were exceeded at Dairy Creek at Highway 8 near Hillsboro, Oregon, during May 2002 to September 2004.

Total Suspended Solids

Models for the autosampler-only data and the Clean Water Services ambient monitoring data were selected for high flow and the first routine samples from each month (the presumed best calibration data available) (table 13). Adjusted-R^2 values were similar in models from Scenarios 1 and 2 (0.695–0.758). However, coefficients of determination for the goodness-of-fit validations were poor, less than 0.2 for all models. Bias correction factors were 1.02–1.03 for all models. Seasonal factors evaluated by inclusion of sine and cosine terms were insignificant and models using them are not shown.

Turbidity was an important explanatory variable for all models in both scenarios. In Scenario 1, the addition of discharge as an independent variable caused small increases in the adjusted R^2 in Models 2 and 4 over Models 1 and 3. However, the addition of discharge generally increased the error when predicted values were compared to the validation dataset. The addition of discharge also increased the level of multicollinearity, with VIFs for both turbidity and discharge exceeding the calculated VIF_{crit} in Model 4. In contrast, the addition of discharge to Scenario 2 models had little effect on the calibration of the models, provided only a minor benefit to the models' validation, and incurred possible multicollinearity in Model 6. High stages were not experienced during the autosampler deployments so discharge data were available and meaningful for all the Scenario 1 samples. However, stages greater than 10 ft were recorded for several samples in the Scenario 2 dataset. No discharge data were available for these samples from high stages, which explains the lack of benefit of discharge as an explanatory variable for TSS in Models 6 and 8.

The inclusion of specific conductance data was not statistically significant for any Scenario 1 or 2 models, and reduced the fit in almost all cases. The model coefficients for turbidity were the same in Models 1 and 3 (a = 0.025), and in Models 2 and 4 (a = 0.019), regardless of the addition of specific conductance, with similar effects in Scenario 2.

Scenario 2 may represent the most robust input datasets available for Dairy Creek, and Models 5 or 6, therefore, may represent reasonable initial models for TSS, although their respective goodness-of-fit statistics were poor. Models 5 and 6 provide similar results (hence, Model 6 is not shown in figure 14), and capture the baseline conditions (about 10 mg/L) moderately well for some periods in each summer during 2002–04. Model 1, derived from autosampler-only data and, therefore, limited by the range of conditions observed and by serial-correlation issues, overestimates the baseline conditions more than Models 5 or 6, especially when the actual TSS values drop to less than about 8 mg/L. Model 1 also has much greater variability and higher peak values than Models 5 or 6.

Results from the Scenario 1 and Scenario 2 models indicate that the most robust model form for TSS at Dairy Creek will probably be log$TSS= f$ (*Turbidity*), although the addition of discharge (or stage) may be beneficial, especially at high discharges. Backwater issues will make discharge a difficult variable to use in the winter. Although stage data remain accurate during backwater conditions, the presence of these conditions still may require development of separate models for free-flowing and backwater conditions. Assuming that Scenario 2 uses more representative and thorough datasets than Scenario 1, the presumed best model for TSS at Dairy Creek, given the available data, is currently Model 5. Model 5 may appear to underestimate TSS during base flow (fig. 14), but this is an artifact of the superposition of the Model 1 results onto the graph, where the Model 5 line is obscured by the Model 1 line. The base-flow calibration and validation data are relatively well represented by the Model 5 results, and furthermore they are well within the 95 percent prediction interval for Model 5. Given this, Model 5 may perform adequately during summer.

A comparison of predicted and measured TSS concentrations from Model 5 (fig. 15) further illustrates the predominance in the Scenario 2 dataset by samples at relatively low TSS concentrations. Most measured concentrations were in the range of $10^{0.6}$ (or about 4.0) to $10^{1.5}$ (or about 32) mg/L, Importantly, this comparison also reveals the relatively large uncertainty of the model, with prediction intervals that encompass about a full order of magnitude. The clustering of predicted values at about $10^{1.0}$ (or about 10) mg/L despite a moderate range in measured values likely is an indication that a model based on turbidity alone is insensitive to some of the factors contributing to raised TSS, and that inclusion of other independent variables such as stage or discharge or separation of models based on a stage threshold such as 10 ft will be beneficial.

Table 13. Preliminary model statistics for correlation of total suspended solids with continuous parameters at Dairy Creek at Highway 8 near Hillsboro, Oregon, 2002–04.

[Regression models are of the form $TSS = a*Turb + b*Q + c*SC + d$, where a, b, and c are model coefficients and d is the intercept, $Turb$, Q, and SC are the explanatory variables turbidity (in Formazin Nephelometric Units), discharge (in cubic feet per second), and specific conductance (in microsiemens per centimeter), respectively, and TSS is the dependent variable, total suspended solids, in milligrams per liter. Where TSS is log transformed, a bias transformation factor (BCF; Duan, 1983) is multiplied by $10^{(logTSS)}$ to get the final value. The maximum Variance Inflation Factor (VIF) indicates the largest VIF obtained for any one variable in the correlation. **Abbreviations:** n, number of samples; Adj.-R^2, adjusted R^2, a coefficient of determination which adjusts for degrees of freedom and penalizes the use of too many explanatory variables; f, a function of indicated constituents; log, base 10 logarithm; RMSE, root mean square error; –, not included in the regression]

Model No. and form	Model calibration								Model validation—Goodness-of-fit evaluation				
	Value of coefficient, when used					Correlation statistics			Mean error	Validation RMSE	Coefficient of determination	Nash-Sutcliffe coefficient	z-statistic from sign test
	a	b	c	d	BCF	n	Adj.-R^2	Maximum VIF					
Scenario 1	Calibration data set— Autosamplers only								Validation data set— Clean Water Services ambient monitoring data				
1. logTSS=f($Turb$)	0.025	–	–	0.709	1.03	38	0.704	–	-2.2	5	0.07	-0.16	3.5
2. logTSS=f($Turb$, Q)	0.019	0.002	–	0.642	1.02	38	0.745	2.1	-3.9	6.1	0.10	-0.57	5.2
3. logTSS=f($Turb$, SC)	0.025	–	0.0009	0.696	1.03	38	0.695	1.4	-2.2	5	0.06	-0.17	3.5
4. logTSS=f($Turb$, Q, SC)	0.019	0.002	0.0009	0.524	1.02	38	0.738	[1]2.3	-4	6.3	0.03	-0.64	5
Scenario 2	Calibration data set— Peak autosampler plus first monthly and high flow monitoring samples from Clean Water Services dataset								Validation data set— Remaining monthly Clean Water Services ambient monitoring + non-peak autosampler data				
5. logTSS=f($Turb$)	0.051	–	–	0.415	1.02	20	0.758	–	0.07	4.6	0.06	0.06	2.5
6. logTSS=f($Turb$, Q)	0.051	0.0001	–	0.396	1.02	20	0.757	[1]2.7	-0.49	4.9	0.13	0.08	1
7. logTSS=f($Turb$, SC)	0.053	–	0.0007	0.304	1.02	20	0.754	1.1	-1.4	4.6	0.14	0.04	1.3
8. logTSS=f($Turb$, Q, SC)	0.054	0.0002	0.0009	0.251	1.02	20	0.758	1.3	-1.5	4.9	0.19	0.11	1.6

[1]Exceeds a threshold VIF value, calculated as $\{1/(1-(\text{Adj.-}R^2)\}$ and indicates possible multicollinearity.

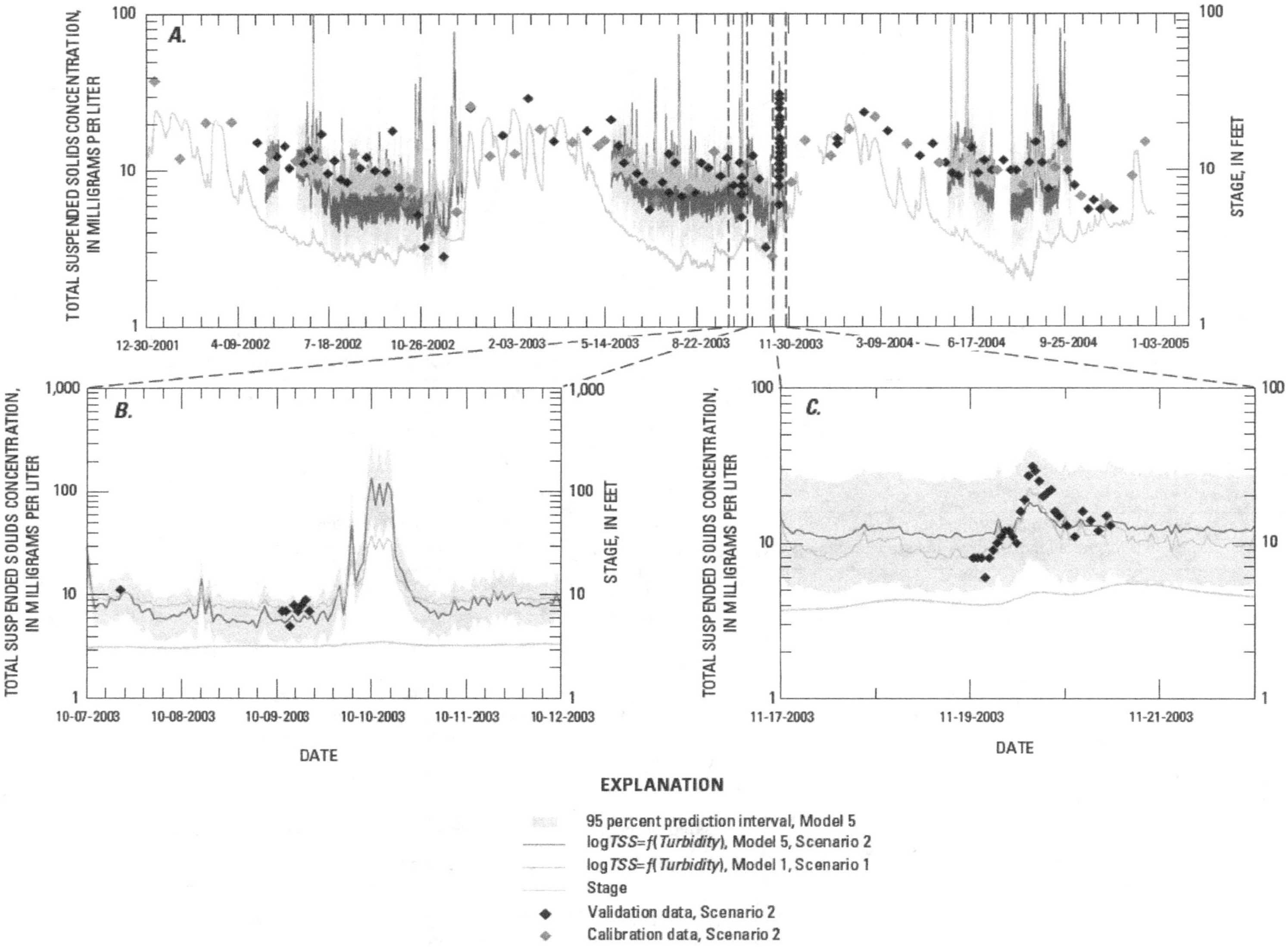

Figure 14. Time series of predicted total suspended solid (TSS) concentrations at Dairy Creek at Highway 8 near Hillsboro, from Models 1 and 5, with prediction intervals, calibration, and validation data (*A*) during 2002–04, (*B*) during storm 1, and (*C*) during storm 2, Tualatin River basin, Oregon. Winter conditions are not predicted because of the lack of available monitor and discharge data.

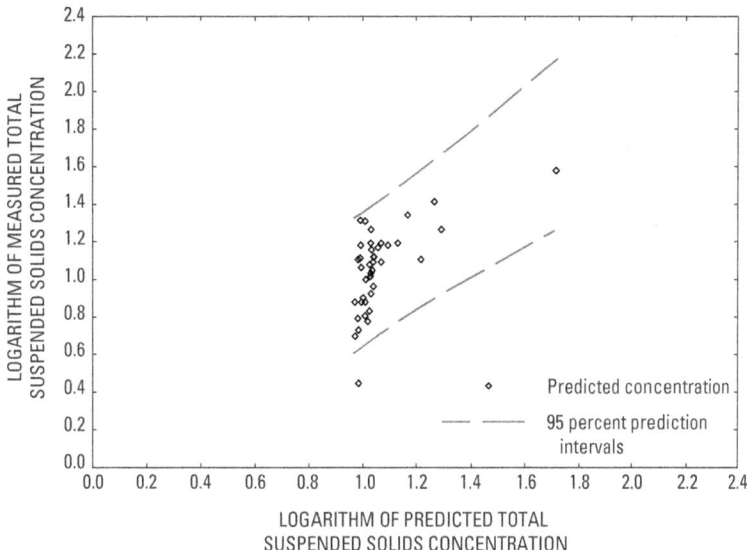

Figure 15. Comparison of predicted and measured concentrations of total suspended solids from Model 5 for Dairy Creek at Highway 8 near Hillsboro, Oregon. Native reporting units for total suspended solids concentrations prior to log transformation were in milligrams per liter.

Total Phosphorus

Models for TP at Dairy Creek from Scenario 1 were primarily dependent on turbidity, with discharge and specific conductance playing a lesser role. Using the Scenario 2 data, however, each model includes specific conductance which exerts a stronger role than either turbidity or discharge (table 14), and which may be a result of the more expansive range of specific conductances encompassed by the Scenario 2 dataset. Sine and cosine terms again were insignificant, suggesting that seasonal considerations were unimportant or already incorporated with the other independent variables. Coefficients of determination (adjusted-R^2) for calibration of Scenario 1, Models 1 and 2, were substantially better than those from all other models examined, regardless of input datasets, potentially owing to serial correlation. Coefficients for turbidity in Scenario 1 ranged from 0.012 to 0.021, and coefficients for discharge and specific conductance were an order of magnitude less, varying little between models where they were used. Bias correction factors were relatively low, ranging from 1.01 to 1.04 among all models and both scenarios.

In Scenario 2, coefficients for specific conductance were essentially unchanged (0.003–0.004) between models, and were slightly less than one half the value of the respective Scenario 1 models (0.009). The number of observations (n) in the Scenario 2 models were, for the most part, fewer than those used in the Fanno Creek models (Scenarios 2 and 3, table 11). The number of observations was less because the Scenario 2 dataset includes many samples from mid-winter during 2002–04, when stage in Dairy Creek was greater than 10 ft (discharge unavailable), and (or) the continuous monitor at the Dairy Creek site had been removed for the winter. The use of stage as an explanatory variable in Scenario 2, in place of discharge, allowed the inclusion of eight additional samples in the calibration dataset but resulted in a lower adjusted-R^2 for the model.

On the basis of calibration and validation statistics, no model from either scenario is strong enough for predictive purposes. Mean errors are relatively small, especially for Scenario 2 models. Possible multicollinearity was indicated for Models 1, 3, and 8, although the maximum VIFs were relatively low. Coefficients of determination for the model validation exercise were highest (0.55) for Model 1, and were otherwise poor (<0.1–0.38) for all other models.

Table 14.   Preliminary model statistics for correlation of total phosphorus with continuous parameters at Dairy Creek at Highway 8 near Hillsboro, Oregon, 2002–04.

[Regression models are of the form $TP = a*Turb + b*Q + c*SC + d$, where a, b, and c are model coefficients and d is the intercept, $Turb$, Q, and SC are the explanatory variables turbidity (in Formazin Nephelometric Units), discharge (in cubic feet per second), and specific conductance (in microsiemens per centimeter), respectively, and TP is the dependent variable, total phosphorus, in milligrams per liter. Where TP is log transformed, a bias transformation factor (BCF; Duan, 1983) is multiplied by $10^{(logTP)}$ to get the final value. Data sets for correlation included peak discharge samples from the autosampler deployment, plus monthly and high flow monitoring samples from Clean Water Services databases. Stage is used in place of discharge with the Clean Water Services data because discharge data are not provided by Oregon Water Resources Department when stage is greater than 10 feet. RMSE values are in milligrams per liter. The maximum Variance Inflation Factor (VIF) indicates the largest VIF obtained for any one variable in the correlation. **Abbreviations:** n, number of samples; Adj.-R^2, adjusted R^2, a coefficient of determination which adjusts for degrees of freedom and penalizes the use of too many explanatory variables; f, a function of indicated constituents; log, base 10 logarithm; RMSE, root mean square error; –, not included in the regression]

Model No. and form	Model calibration — Value of coefficient, when used					Correlation statistics			Model validation – Goodness-of-fit evaluation				
	a	b	c	d	BCF	n	Adj.-R^2	Maximum VIF	Mean error	Validation RMSE	Coefficient of determination	Nash-Sutcliffe coefficient	z-statistic from sign test
Scenario 1	Calibration data set— Autosamplers only								Validation data set— Clean Water Services ambient monitoring data				
1. $logTP$=f($Turb$, Q, SC)	0.021	-0.0008	0.009	-2.26	1.01	37	0.808	[1]2.9	0.023	0.06	0.55	-2.1	0.49
2. $logTP$=f($Turb$, SC)	0.018	–	0.009	-2.32	1.01	37	0.788	1.3	0.015	0.1	0.38	-4.9	1.8
3. $logTP$=f($Turb$, Q)	0.017	-0.001	–	-1	1.01	37	0.535	[1]2.7	0.025	0.05	0.08	-0.86	3.5
4. $logTP$=f($Turb$)	0.012	–	–	-1.03	1.02	37	0.503	–	0.005	0.04	0.00	-0.09	2
Scenario 2	Calibration data set— Peak autosampler plus first monthly and high flow monitoring samples from Clean Water Services dataset								Validation data set—Remaining monthly Clean Water Services ambient monitoring + non-peak autosampler data				
5. $logTP$=f(SC)	–	–	0.003	-1.35	1.01	19	0.557	–	-0.001	0.04	0.27	0.26	2.2
6. $logTP$=f($Turb$, SC)	-0.012	–	0.004	-1.32	1.01	30	0.711	1.0	-0.0006	0.04	0.15	0.07	3.2
7. $logTP$=f(Q, SC)[2]	–	-0.00007	0.004	-1.44	1.02	31	0.683	1.1	-0.0008	0.03	0.18	0.14	3.2
8. $logTP$=f($Stage$, SC)[3]	–	0.004	0.004	-1.45	1.04	39	0.375	[1]1.4	-0.002	0.03	0.20	0.17	1.6
9. $logTP$=f($Turb$, $Stage$, SC)	-0.006	-0.007	0.003	-1.22	1.01	19	0.533	1.2	-0.002	0.04	0.04	-0.1	2.9

[1] Exceeds a threshold VIF value, calculated as {1/(1 – (Adj.-R^2)}; and indicates possible multicollinearity.

[2] High discharge (and accompanying samples) excluded, where stage greater than 10 feet.

[3] High stage data available. Note increase in number of samples. Residuals wide-spread for high stage samples.

Many of the Nash-Sutcliffe coefficients were near zero or negative (max = 0.26), indicating that the means of the laboratory data may be as good a predictor as the models derived from it. The goodness-of-fit statistics are more reflective of base flow than high-flow conditions because of the paucity of high-flow data, especially for the validation dataset; therefore, model performance could not be properly evaluated. Additional data would be needed to refine and evaluate the models.

The predicted results of Scenario 2 models for TP at Dairy Creek captured the general seasonal pattern of summer baseline concentrations relatively well, but did not appear to capture the shorter term variability associated with events or other factors (fig. 16). Although Scenario 2 is assumed to represent a more robust calibration scheme than Scenario 1, Model 1 results tracked better with the laboratory data from the Storm 2 hydrograph than either Model 5 or Model 7, and may better represent the range of variability experienced under normal conditions. Model 1 also predicted high storm peaks of TP, sometimes exceeding 1 mg/L, but the accuracy of these predictions could not be evaluated. Results from Model 8, which incorporate stage rather than discharge, are not shown in figure 16 because they were almost identical to those of Model 7. Likewise, Model 6 (not shown in figure 16), the highest ranked model from Scenario 2 that used turbidity, did not capture the Storm 2 increases in TP and produced only minor variations compared to Models 5–8.

Comparisons of measured and predicted TP values for Model 1 have less variability and stay within the prediction intervals better than the values for Model 5 (fig. 17). Model 6 results were similar to those from Model 5. However, Model 1 used input data from Scenario 1 and Model 5 used input data from Scenario 2, so the two models are not directly comparable.

Generally, Scenario 1 models, particularly Model 1, were slightly more useful than those from Scenario 2 for estimating TP concentrations at Dairy Creek, but no model provided acceptably accurate predictions using the available datasets. Model 1 may overestimate variability in stream TP concentrations, but could be useful for understanding the overall pattern of TP resulting from changes in streamflow, turbidity, or specific conductance. However, it must be stressed that maximum TP concentrations encompassed by the Scenario 1 input data were less than 0.25 mg/L, so the model cannot be relied upon for predictions of concentrations greater than 0.25 mg/L. Furthermore, the reliance on discharge will be a limitation during high stages unless backwater conditions are comprehensively understood at the Dairy Creek site at Highway 8. The inclusion of specific conductance in almost every model implies that much of the TP in Dairy Creek may come from dissolved sources or may be associated with the movement of solutes in the basin, which is consistent with known groundwater inputs of dissolved phosphorus to Tualatin River basin streams during summer. Alternatively, because specific conductance is sometimes correlated with discharge, its presence in the models might also reflect erosion and solute sources, including phosphorus, at higher flows.

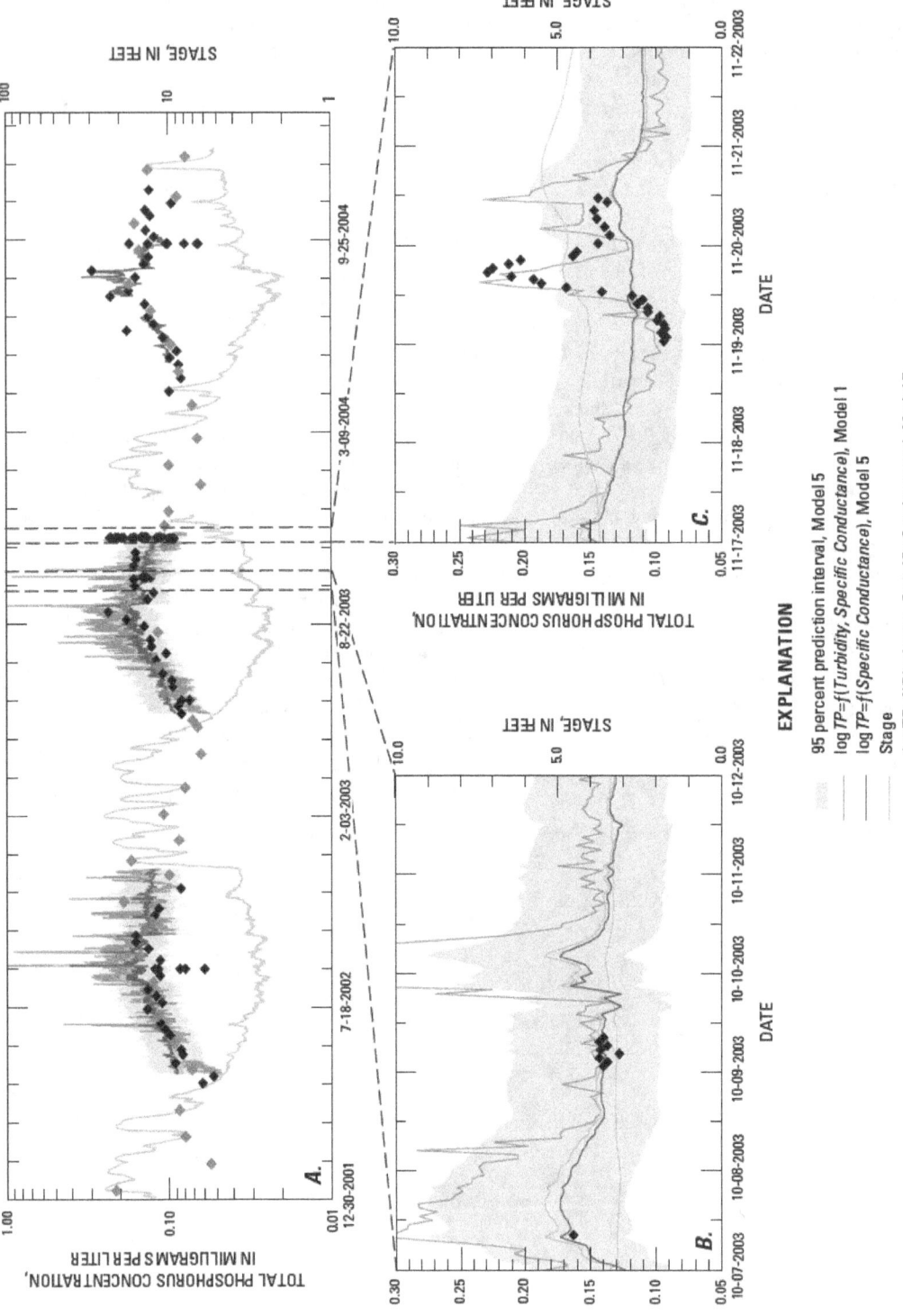

Figure 16. Time series of predicted total phosphorus concentrations at Dairy Creek at Highway 8 near Hillsboro, from Models 1, 5, and 7, with prediction intervals, calibration, and validation data (*A*) during 2002–04, (*B*) during storm 1, and (*C*) during storm 2, Tualatin River basin, Oregon. Winter conditions are not predicted because of the lack of available monitor and discharge data.

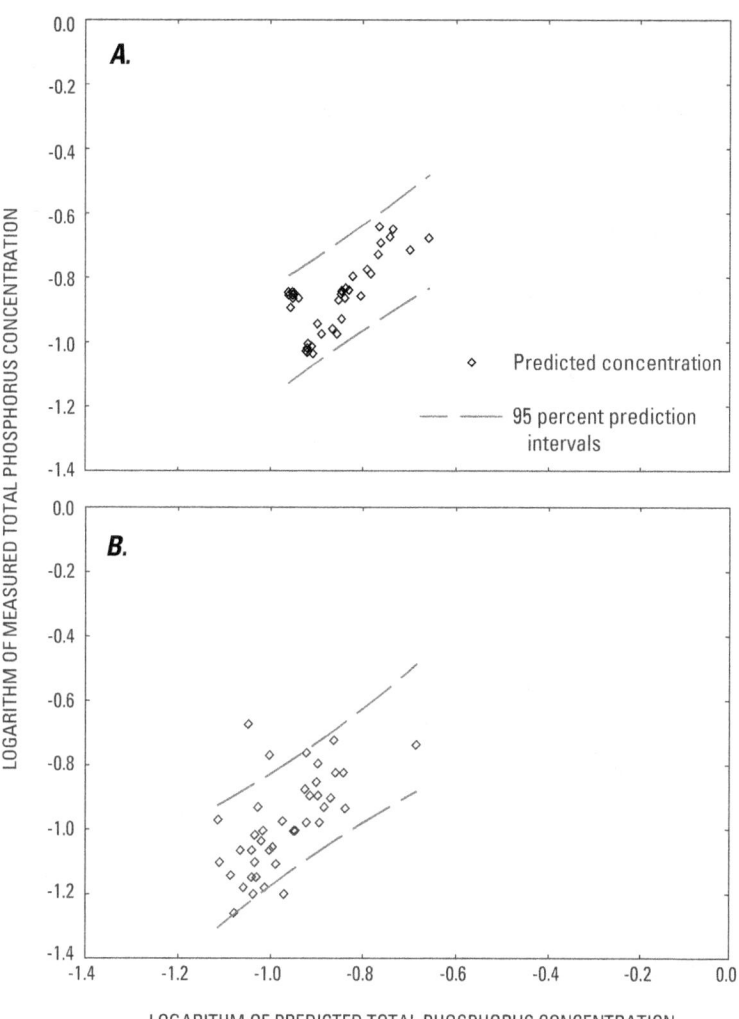

Figure 17.   Comparison of measured and predicted total phosphorus concentrations at Dairy Creek at Highway 8 near Hillsboro, from (*A*) Scenario 1, Model 1, and (*B*) Scenario 2, Model 5, Tualatin River basin, Oregon. Native reporting units for total phosphorus concentrations prior to log transformation were in milligrams per liter.

Escherichia coli Bacteria

Models for *E. coli* bacteria at Dairy Creek were primarily functions of specific conductance; only Model 4 in Scenario 1, using the autosampler data, did not include specific conductance (table 15). Furthermore, seasonal aspects were unimportant, with sine and cosine terms again being insignificant. The coefficients for specific conductance varied little between the individual models within a specified scenario, ranging from -0.025 to -0.029 for Scenario 1 models, and from 0.011 to 0.013 for Scenario 2 models. Coefficients for specific conductance were negative in Scenario 1 and positive in Scenario 2, suggesting that the response of *E. coli* bacteria during the storms sampled by autosamplers in autumn 2003 was different than in the long term Scenario 2 dataset. Multicollinearity, which can result in coefficients with signs different than expected, may have contributed to the results of Models 7b or 8, despite the low maximum VIFs of 1.4 and 1.2, respectively. The low VIF_{crit} values for these models reflect the poor adjusted-R^2 values for the Scenario 2 dataset—all VIF values are well below the general rule-of-thumb values sometimes used by other investigators (Helsel and Hirsch, 1992); likewise the Condition Index (not shown), an alternate measure of multicolinearity (Draper and Smith, 1998) was about 50 for Models 1 and 3 but less than 20 for Models 6 and 7, in the range previously described as acceptable (Draper and Smith, 1988).

Although bacteria often are associated with particles in streams, *E. coli* bacteria regression models resulting from this study were only a function of turbidity in a few cases, primarily from Scenario 1. Log transformation introduced substantial bias when predicting *E. coli* bacteria, resulting in BCF values for Scenario 2 models from 1.29 to 1.45, indicating corrections of about 29 to 45 percent. Scenario 1 BCFs were lower (1.05–1.12) than those in Scenario 2, but remain mostly higher than for TP (table 14) and TSS (table 13). Comparatively high BCFs were also determined for *E. coli* bacteria models for Fanno Creek (table 12).

Adjusted-R^2 values for calibration of Scenario 1 models for *E. coli* bacteria were substantially greater than for Scenario 2 models, which was also the case for models for TSS and TP. In contrast, model validation statistics, particularly the coefficients of determination and the Nash-Sutcliffe coefficients, were all poor. None of the models' validation statistics were within the optimal ranges for errors generated by the prediction of *E. coli* bacteria counts. The highest Nash-Sutcliffe coefficient was only 0.21 for the Scenario 2 model using stage instead of discharge (Model 7b) as an independent variable, and all the coefficients of determination were less than or equal to 0.1.

The negative coefficients for specific conductance from the Scenario 1 models were opposite in direction to those from Scenario 2. As a consequence, the pattern from models using specific conductance in Scenario 1 also were opposite in direction to those from Scenario 2. All models overestimated bacteria counts in storm 1 (fig. 18). Data collection for storm 1 preceded the largest stream response by about 1 day, although Model 4, which was a function of turbidity only, predicted bacteria counts that were closest to the measured values. Model 1 (not shown), with a negative coefficient for specific conductance, predicted summer *E. coli* counts that were below the baseline and were not realistic. Model 4 also performed better during storm 2 than either Scenario 2 model shown (fig. 18C), mimicking the temporary increases in bacteria counts during the storm. Models 5 and 7b were selected for plotting because they represented the best Scenario 2 calibration model according to the Mallow's Cp selection scheme and the best validation according to the Nash-Sutcliffe coefficients, respectively. Both models performed almost identically; the line from either model obscures the other in figure 18, reflecting the influence of specific conductance as an independent variable.

Comparison of measured and predicted values for *E. coli* bacteria models show considerable variation and generally poor predictions, especially by Model 5 (fig. 19B). Uncertainty around Model 5 was greater than for Model 4, particularly at low and high bacteria counts. Neither model demonstrated acceptable abilities to reproduce the measured values; all models should be considered preliminary. It is possible that the sources and dynamics of *E. coli* bacteria in Dairy Creek cannot be well characterized by variables such as flow, stage, specific conductance, and turbidity. If so, then this approach of using continuous monitors to estimate *E. coli* bacteria concentrations in Dairy Creek may fail. More data are needed to make such a conclusion.

Given the model calibration and validation statistics, and the performance of the models at predicting time series data and reproducing the original measured values used in the correlations, reliable predictions for *E. coli* bacteria at Dairy Creek at Highway 8 is a possibility, but several challenges remain. Although the continuous monitor at that site was converted to a permanent installation in 2004, the potential for backwater at stages greater than 10 ft during winter causes several concerns. Stage instead of discharge may be required as an explanatory variable, and separate models may be needed for winter and for summer. *E. coli* bacteria (and other constituents) may respond differently to backwater conditions than to unimpeded flow conditions, including potential issues of particle settling or upstream sources. One potential problem with backwater, the introduction of water from the downstream receiving waters at the sampling location, does not occur at the Highway 8 site (C. Beaman, Oregon Water Resources Department, written commun., April 22, 2009).

Table 15. Preliminary model statistics for correlation of *Escherichia coli* bacteria with continuous parameters at Dairy Creek at Highway 8 near Hillsboro, Oregon, 2002–04.

[Regression models are of the form $E.\ coli = a*Turb+ b*Q + c*SC + d$, where a, b, and c are model coefficients and d is the intercept, *Turb*, *Q*, and *SC* are the explanatory variables turbidity (in Formazin Nephelometric Units), discharge (in cubic feet per second), and specific conductance (in microsiemens per centimeter), respectively, and *E. coli* is the dependent variable, in colonies per 100 milliliters. Where *E. coli* is log transformed, a bias transformation factor (BCF; Duan, 1983) is multiplied by $10^{(logE.coli)}$ to get the final value. Model 7b was not included in the model selection scheme because stage and discharge are surrogates for one another, but model 7b was built separately to evaluate the use of stage as an independent variable to compensate for backwater effects on discharge at the Dairy Creek site. RMSE values are in colonies per 100 milliliters. The maximum Variance Inflation Factor (VIF) indicates the largest VIF obtained for any one variable in the correlation. **Abbreviations:** *E. coli*, *Escherichia coli* bacteria; *n*, number of samples; Adj.-R^2, adjusted R^2, a coefficient of determination which adjusts for degrees of freedom and penalizes the use of too many explanatory variables; f, a function of indicated constituents; log, base 10 logarithm; RMSE, root mean square error; NA, VIFs are not applicable because only one independent variable was used]

Model No. and form	Model calibration — Value of coefficient, when used					Correlation statistics			Model validation—Goodness-of-fit evaluation				
	a	b	c	d	BCF	n	Adj.-R^2	Maximum VIF	Mean error	Validation RMSE	Coefficient of determination	Nash-Sutcliffe coefficient	z-statistic from sign test
Scenario 1	**Calibration data set—Autosamplers only**								**Validation data set—Clean Water Services ambient monitoring data**				
1. log*E. coli* =f(*Turb, SC*)	0.035	—	-0.025	5.14	1.05	37	0.871	1.3	185	694	0.10	-4.1	0.31
2. log*E. coli* =f(*Turb, Q, SC*)	0.036	-0.0001	-0.025	5.15	1.05	37	0.867	2.9	118	735	0.09	-3.3	0.63
3. log*E. coli* =f(*Q, SC*)	—	0.005	-0.029	5.71	1.12	38	0.715	1.2	11	653	0.10	-2.4	1.1
4. log*E. coli* =f(*Turb*)	0.049	—	—	1.69	1.1	37	0.695	NA	-122	331	0.01	-0.15	0.93
Scenario 2	**Calibration data set—Peak autosampler plus first monthly and high flow monitoring samples from Clean Water Services dataset**								**Validation data set—Remaining monthly Clean Water Services ambient monitoring + non-peak autosampler data**				
5. log*E. coli* =f(*SC*)	—	—	0.013	0.713	1.29	17	0.342	NA	94	567	0.02	-3.2	1.2
6. log*E. coli* =f(*Turb, SC*)	0.017	—	0.013	0.497	1.45	17	0.309	1.0	161	667	0.03	-4.8	2.4
7a. log*E. coli* =f(*Q, SC*)	—	-0.0004	0.011	0.981	1.37	16	0.378	1.2	19	329	0.02	0.13	1.8
7b. log*E. coli* =f(*Stage, SC*)	—	-0.0001	0.011	0.828	1.36	32	0.391	[1]1.4	-2	331	0.02	0.21	0.9
8. log*E. coli* =f(*Turb, Q, SC*)	0.017	0.00001	0.013	0.494	1.45	17	0.256	[1]1.2	71	338	0.07	-0.26	2

[1] Exceeds a threshold VIF value, calculated as $\{1/(1-(Adj.-R^2))\}$ and indicates possible multicollinearity.

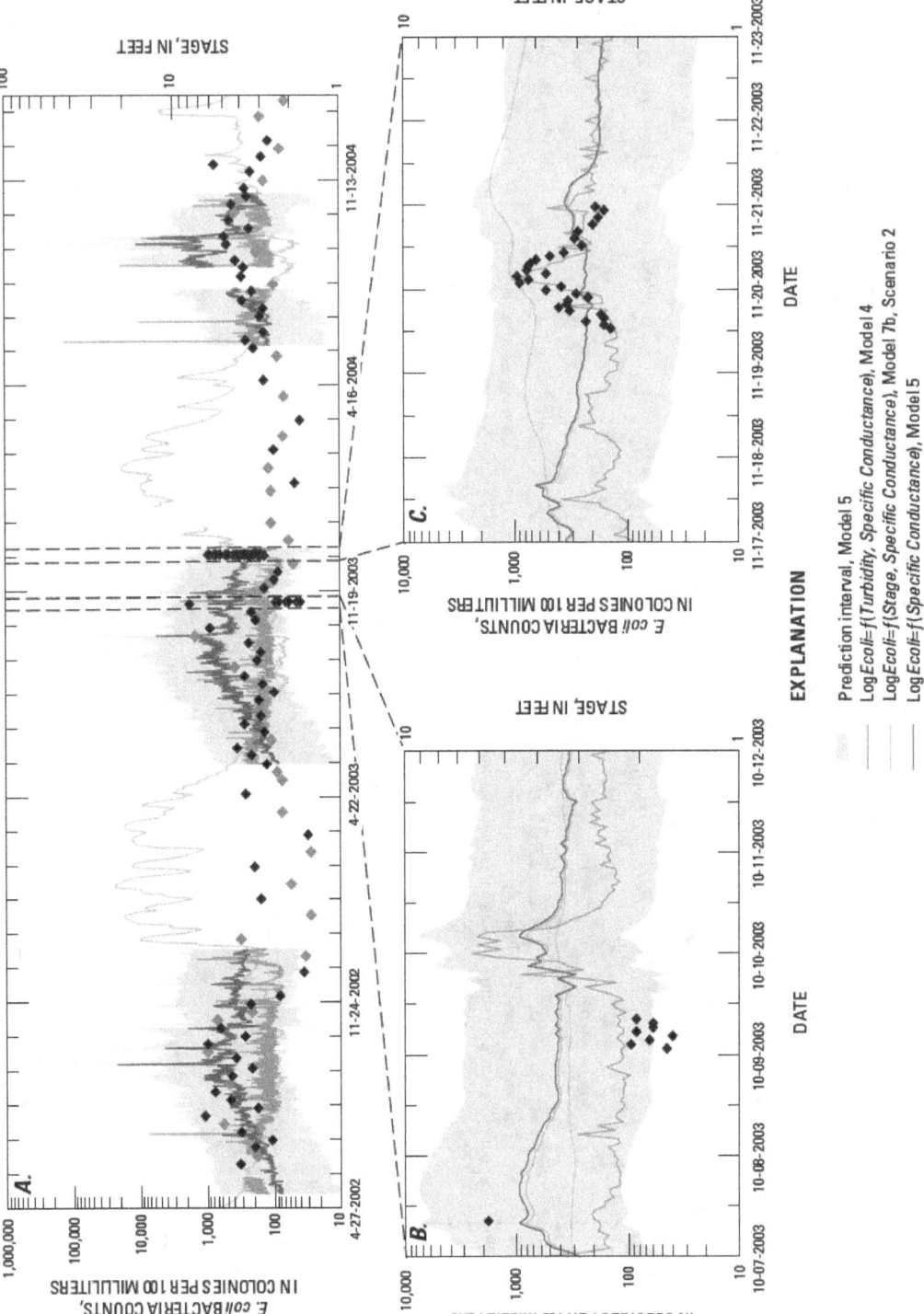

EXPLANATION

Prediction interval, Model 5

LogEcoli=f(Turbidity, Specific Conductance), Model 4

LogEcoli=f(Stage, Specific Conductance), Model 7b, Scenario 2

LogEcoli=f(Specific Conductance), Model 5

Stage

◆ Calibration data, Scenario 2

◆ Validation data, Scenario 2

Figure 18. Time series of predicted *Escherichia coli* (*E. coli*) bacteria concentrations at Dairy Creek at Highway 8 near Hillsboro, from Models 4, 5, and 7b, with prediction intervals, calibration, and validation data (*A*) during 2002–04 , (*B*) during storm 1, and (*C*) during storm 2, Tualatin River basin, Oregon. Winter conditions are not predicted because of the lack of available monitor and discharge data.

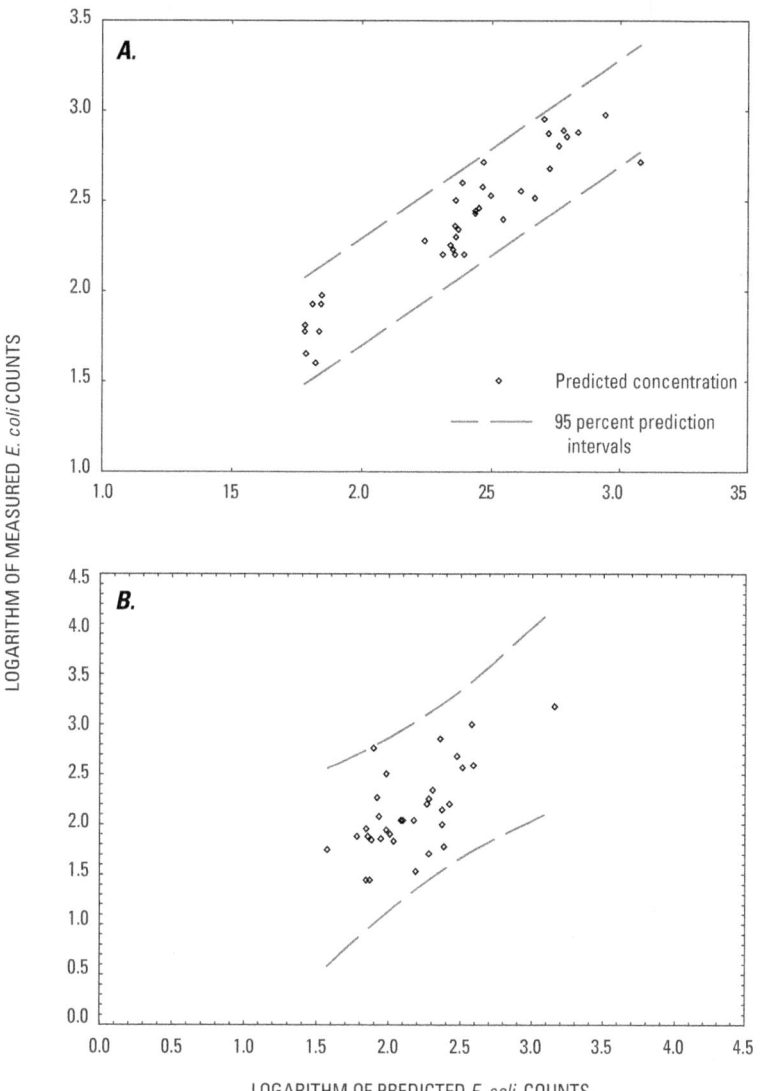

Figure 19. Comparison of measured and predicted *Escherichia coli* (*E. coli*) bacteria counts using (*A*) Model 4 and (*B*) Model 5, Dairy Creek at Highway 8 near Hillsboro, Oregon. Native reporting units for *E. coli* bacteria counts prior to log transformation were in colonies per 100 milliliters.

Non-Target Sites

Preliminary model forms were identified for TSS, TP, and *E. coli* bacteria at the non-target sites using autosampler-only data (table 16) and minimization of Mallow's Cp. Other than removal of outliers that cannot be resolved, and log-transformation of dependent variables, no attempt was made to verify homoscedasticity, use additional data, compensate for autocorrelation, or otherwise optimize the models. Model coefficients and adjusted-R^2 values are not shown because the objective of this exercise was to evaluate the likelihood that models that are more robust could be developed if data representative of the range of environmental conditions at these sites become available.

Table 16.   Preliminary functional model forms for total suspended solids, total phosphorus, and *Escherichia coli* bacteria at non-target tributary sites in the Tualatin River basin, Oregon, 2002–04.

[Model forms are based on autosampler-only data If the adjusted-R^2 of the optimum model, based on minimization of Mallow's Cp, was greater than 0 5, then the functional form of the optimal model is shown, without model coefficients If the adjusted-R^2 was less than 0 5, then no model is shown and the result is listed as N/A (not applicable) *Turb*, *Q*, and *SC* are the explanatory variables of turbidity (in Formazin Nephelometric Units), discharge (in cubic feet per second), and specific conductance (in microsiemens per centimeter), respectively **Abbreviations:** *TSS*, total suspended solids; *TP*, total phosphorus; *E. coli*, *Escherichia coli* bacteria; log, base 10 logarithm; f, a function of indicated constituents]

Site	Functional model form		
	TSS	**TP**	***E. coli***
Beaverton Creek at SW 170th Ave.	logTSS=f($Turb$,SC,Q)	logTP=f($Turb$,SC,Q)	N/A
Chicken Creek at Scholls-Sherwood Highway	logTSS=f($Turb$,SC,Q)	logTP=f($Turb$,SC,Q)	N/A
Rock Creek at Woll Pond Way near Hillsboro	logTSS=f($Turb$,SC,Q)	logTP=f(SC,Q)	N/A
Gales Creek at Old Highway 47	logTSS=f($Turb$,SC,Q)	logTP=f($Turb$,SC,Q)	log$E.$ $coli$=f($Turb$,SC,Q)

Results in table 16 indicate a high probability that robust regression models can be developed for TSS and TP at all non-target sites, but that *E. coli* bacteria may be difficult to predict at sites other than Gales Creek at Old Highway 47. In almost all other cases, models of the form log$X$= f ($Turb$, SC, Q), where X is the dependent variable, may be constructed and would provide acceptable predictions. For the Rock Creek site, a regression model with specific conductance and discharge may be sufficient to predict logTP. When *E. coli* bacteria model results are not applicable, the adjusted-R^2 values of the functional models were much lower than 0.5 as indicated in table 16; most were less than 0.1, and the available data were insufficient for predicting *E. coli* bacteria. The adjusted-R^2 values for all other indicated models were greater than 0.7, which in some cases indicate even stronger correlations than the models for Fanno and Dairy Creeks. However, some of the limitations of the available data and the stream responses at the non-target sites should be considered:

1. Discharge (and stage) was not continuously measured at either the Rock Creek or Beaverton Creek sites, so instantaneous values at those sites were reconstructed by simple routing of upstream discharges at existing stream gages. Considerable error likely was inherent in the timing and magnitude of the resulting hourly estimates of the storm hydrographs, especially considering the dynamic and variable nature of stream responses to different storms.

2. No large storms were sampled at Chicken Creek, where the relatively undeveloped drainage basin muted the stream response to storms. Indeed, the stream response may represent an increase in groundwater input after storms rather than direct runoff, as indicated by minimal increases in turbidity and increases (rather than the expected decreases) in specific conductance. Nonetheless, Chicken Creek does, at times, respond to large storms, and warrants future study.

3. Storm responses at the Gales Creek site were more muted than at several of the other sites and had lower flows than originally intended, and the range of values of the potential explanatory variables (turbidity, discharge, and specific conductance) was small.

4. The Rock Creek at Woll Pond Way site was just downstream of an anomalous sediment source, where the streambank was observed to episodically calve into the river during high flow and cause short-term pulses of high turbidity that may have been poorly mixed. It is likely that the turbidity and sediment response at this site were not necessarily reflective of larger drainage basin processes. Subsequent to this study, the monitor at the Rock Creek site was moved downstream to a bridge crossing and reinstalled with a more permanent (all-season) design, so any attempt to predict water quality in Rock Creek would benefit from collection of data at the new site.

Given these limitations, additional efforts to further refine the model results at the non-target sites are not warranted without additional data collection specifically from high flow conditions and during several seasonal periods. Nonetheless, preliminary results in this study indicate that reasonably robust models for some constituents can be developed if appropriate data become available.

Discussion

The use of continuously measured parameters as surrogates for unmeasured constituents, including real-time applications, has increased in recent years. Rasmussen and others (2008) published regression models for 19 constituents, including whole-water and dissolved solutes such as various major ions (calcium, magnesium, and sulfate) nutrients, and bacteria (bacteria, fecal coliform, and enterococcus) at 5 sites in Kansas. The program in Kansas has been successful enough that results of the regression predictions are posted online in real time, and coefficients of determination for the regression models mostly range from about 0.6 to greater than 0.9. However, the streams in Kansas, which are known to consistently carry appreciable sediment loads and to have relatively steady flow, are different from Tualatin River tributaries in Oregon. In the Tualatin River basin, most streams are considerably smaller than the streams monitored in Kansas and many have rapid, short-term responses to rainfall runoff (due to their highly urbanized upstream land uses) or highly variable streamflows (given the prolonged dry climate in summer and prolonged wet periods in winter). It was not clear, therefore, that the modeling approaches taken in Kansas and elsewhere could be successfully applied in the Tualatin River basin.

Given the uncertainty over application of the predictive regression techniques to conditions in the Tualatin River tributaries, this study followed a proof-of-concept approach. Regression models and predictions were developed for this report as examples of the type of results that could be obtained for selected Tualatin River tributaries, if additional data were collected to better represent the range of conditions at those sites. Although all the sites (target and non-target) in the study are considered important for management of non-point runoff, the target sites (on Fanno Creek and Dairy Creek) were selected for detailed analysis because they represent land use types (urban and agricultural, respectively) of interest from a management standpoint. Furthermore, additional stream-chemistry data were available for these sites from Clean Water Services (and for Fanno Creek, from USGS) beyond the temporary autosampler deployments used in this study. However, the resulting regression models for these sites are considered preliminary because the available data do not adequately represent the range of conditions expected at these sites, particularly high flows that often lead to high concentrations and loads. Therefore, several models are shown and discussed for each site, any of which could, with sufficient additional data, become the most useful model form for predicting the indicated parameter. Water-quality constituents associated with suspended particulates, notably TSS, TP, and *E. coli* bacteria, were modeled (as dependent variables)

because they are the constituents of greatest interest to local regulators and resource managers, and because they may be most effectively modified through land use management, whereas dissolved constituents such as nitrate or phosphate may be more controlled by groundwater and microbiological processes.

Neither historical dataset (from Clean Water Services and USGS) was originally collected for the purposes used in this report, so neither dataset represented optimal input data for calibration or validation of regression models. High-flow conditions, which in particular cause high concentrations and loads of TSS, TP, and *E. coli* bacteria, are under-represented. The regression models and coefficients discussed in this report, therefore, are considered examples or starting points for future modeling efforts. Furthermore, the aggregation of data from multiple laboratories that was done for Fanno Creek introduced additional uncertainty, particularly for predictions of TSS, for which the input calibration and validation datasets used a combination of TSS analysis from Clean Water Services and suspended sediment concentration analysis from USGS laboratories. No data were available upon which to base any adjustment of USGS suspended sediment concentration data to compare with the TSS analysis by Clean Water Services. Any inherent differences were incorporated into the regression model uncertainties and the magnitude of the prediction intervals.

Several sites in the Tualatin River basin continuously measure streamflow and stream stage, and water-quality monitors collect temperature, specific conductance, dissolved oxygen, pH, and turbidity data, and, at some sites, chlorophyll *a* (see http://or.water.usgs.gov/tualatin/monitors/). Of these, specific conductance, turbidity, and streamflow most directly indicate short-term physical changes in the stream that may result in water-quality changes, and are the most likely candidates to be used as surrogates for water-sample chemical data. Seasonality also was explored with the incorporation of sine and cosine transformations of sample date.

Most results from the regressions for the highly urbanized Fanno Creek site were consistent with findings from Anderson and Rounds (2003), who determined that TSS from three sites in Fanno Creek was significantly correlated with several parameters, including discharge, turbidity, and total dissolved solids (a surrogate for specific conductance). Similarly, TP was significantly correlated with total dissolved solids and turbidity, and *E. coli* bacteria was significantly correlated with turbidity. In this study, models for TSS, TP, and *E. coli* bacteria were primarily a function of turbidity, with discharge and specific conductance typically having various influences on the models. Despite sometimes impressive adjusted-R^2 values for model calibration, the goodness-of-fit statistics from the model validation exercise generally reflected poor agreement with the validation datasets. This poor agreement with the validation datasets was particularly true for the Nash-Sutcliffe coefficient, a measure of model errors that is more stringent than the coefficient of determination for the model. The validation datasets in this study, however, are primarily composed of low-flow samples and do not adequately evaluate the response of the models to high flows, so the actual fit during these conditions is unknown.

Results from Dairy Creek at Highway 8, with primarily undeveloped or agricultural land upstream, were equivocal and likely reflect the limited dataset. No data were available from routine or sporadic studies by the USGS (unlike at Fanno Creek), and no winter data were available for any of the independent variables except stage during 2002–04. Furthermore, backwater conditions at Dairy Creek during late autumn and winter may have a major effect on any correlations that involve discharge and may necessitate separate models for free-flowing as opposed to backwater flow regimes at that site. Using discharge as an independent variable at these high stages would require a different method of stream gaging (for example, measuring stream velocity and deriving a rating for velocity with discharge). Velocity also may be a useful independent variable at this site. The slower velocities associated with backwater produce much less turbulence than the faster velocities associated with unimpeded streamflow thus affecting the quantity of suspended sediment and other particulates. Therefore, correlations of streamflow, turbidity, or specific conductance with TSS, TP, *E. coli* bacteria, and other parameters likely would be different under backwater conditions. The effect of backwater on correlations with dissolved constituents such as orthophosphorus or nitrate-nitrogen may depend on its effect on different sources such as groundwater discharge at high stage. For example, redox or other conditions in temporarily saturated soils could cause changes in the release of nutrients, dissolved minerals, or dissolved organic carbon (which could affect turbidity and specific conductance) if backwater conditions are prolonged.

The lack of significance of sine and cosine terms in any of the regression models may indicate that the other independent variables inherently capture most of the seasonal signal contained in the data. To the extent that seasonal processes such as riparian or upland growth would affect runoff patterns, the continuous records of turbidity, specific conductance, and discharge also should reflect these factors and may more directly measure the indirect seasonal patterns. Additionally, Dairy Creek, with its larger upstream area of agricultural land use and pervious surfaces, generally would be more susceptible to seasonal patterns than Fanno Creek; however, regression modeling was less successful overall at this site than at Fanno Creek. The lack of appropriate high-flow data and difficulties with backwater may have caused problems with the regression-based models at the

Dairy Creek site that masked sine- or cosine-dependent seasonal patterns. Finally, dissolved constituents that are more directly functions of biological processing may be more likely than TSS and TP to exhibit seasonal fluctuations (for example, nitrate production from nitrification, or dissolved orthophosphate uptake during primary production; Anderson and Rounds, 2003). For future modeling efforts, particularly those involving dissolved chemical species, seasonal aspects should be evaluated using sine and cosine terms as independent variables.

Using the Regression Equations

Assuming future development of regression models is successful for some constituents at sites in the Tualatin River basin, the models can be used in several ways. The primary expected use is to evaluate peak concentrations in the modeled streams in response to hydrologic events, and thereby anticipate related water-quality effects or conditions in the mainstem Tualatin River. To fully evaluate effects on the Tualatin River, constituent loads (in mass per year) exported from the tributaries should be calculated or estimated as well; a simple matter if the monitoring station and a streamflow gaging station are located together (for example, Uhrich and Bragg, 2003). Regulators may compare predicted concentrations with benchmarks such as regulatory criteria or TMDL-based requirements, but model uncertainty (for example, the range of possible concentrations indicated by prediction intervals around a given predicted value) should be considered in any such comparison. Water managers may also wish to evaluate predicted concentrations as a potential response of stream restoration or other land-use management changes in the drainage basin. After several years of data collection and iterations of model calibrations, it may be possible to use such models to detect trends in water quality over time. If model coefficients or functional forms change consistently over time in ways that are insensitive to simple increases in the number of samples available for calibration, then such changes could indicate new or reduced sources, steady changes in the association of a particular constituent with another, or other process-based changes in the drainage basin. For example, model forms at a site that are constant for TSS but that have declining coefficients for turbidity in a TP model could indicate that the source of TP has changed and may be less dependent on suspended particulates.

Suggestions for Future Study

The initial plan for this study was to use autosamplers, deployed in conjunction with, and potentially triggered by, continuous monitors to collect high-density data over the course of several storms at individual sites, six of which had been identified in the larger tributaries to the Tualatin River.

These deployments would provide data spanning a broad range of environmental conditions and that could be used to establish initial regression models. The planned sampling was limited, however, by available resources such that only two sites could be sampled for each storm; furthermore, the sampled storms proved to be relatively small and did not produce the desired range of hydrologic responses in the sampled streams. Additional constraints were imposed by limited, seasonal deployments of the continuous monitors at some sites, resulting in fewer continuously monitored data being collected with autosamplers at the highest streamflows. Streamflow or stage was not directly available at two sites (Beaverton and Rock Creeks), and was subject to backwater at another site (Dairy Creek at Highway 8), so only a few measurements were available for use as a surrogate for those sites.

Site Considerations

To build on the findings from this study, several considerations could improve data collection procedures and help select locations at which success would be most likely. These include

1. Permanent or long-term installations of equipment such as streamflow and stream-stage sensors, continuous monitors, and (or) autosamplers, during all seasons and streamflow conditions, and maintenance of stage-discharge rating curves and electronic databases for streamflow and continuous monitors under high and low streamflow conditions. When streamflow cannot be directly monitored at a site, estimation of discharge from upstream or nearby gaging stations requires a more thorough approach than the simple summation and routing that was used at some non-target sites in this study;

2. Availability of telemetry or other remote communication with monitors and autosamplers to enhance the quality of monitor data, reduce downtime, anticipate stream conditions that might result in autosamplers triggering, and allow determination of the status of sample collection. Such communication, together with currently available database software, allows the real-time display of calculated concentrations, loads, and prediction intervals in other locations around the Nation (for example, see http://nrtwq.usgs.gov/ks/);

3. Avoidance of backwater conditions that may render regression models inapplicable under certain situations; alternatively, the development of models that apply seasonally or under specific streamflow conditions;

4. Avoidance of local influences that do not adequately represent drainage basin conditions, but which may exert disproportionately strong influence on water quality at

the sampling or monitoring sites, such as nearby tributary inputs, localized erosion or other sediment sources, point sources, or impoundments.

Samples were collected from Fanno and Dairy Creeks and several additional sites. Regression models were not explored for these additional sites, however, because insufficient storm data were available for 2002-03, or other individual considerations, and because water managers were more interested in Fanno and Dairy Creek. Chicken Creek did not respond readily to storms during the period of study, and seemed to have a groundwater-dominated hydrologic response that resulted in low concentrations of suspended materials. Likewise, Gales Creek at Old Highway 47, with a primarily forested upstream drainage basin, did not show a substantive hydrologic response to storms during periods of monitor deployment. Beaverton and Rock Creeks did not have stream gages at the same sites where the monitors and autosamplers were deployed, and efforts at simple mass-balance routing of streamflow from upstream gaging stations, including tributaries, were unsuccessful for the purposes of this study. Within a short distance upstream of the Rock Creek sampling site, a streambank was actively eroding during high-flows, and that episodic contribution of suspended sediment may not have been representative of upstream sediment and chemistry sources. Although these streams may be subjects of future studies, careful selection of sampling locations and equipment installation will be needed to provide data of sufficient seasonality and quality for successful development of regression models.

Autosamplers

Autosamplers allow the collection of unattended samples during inconvenient times or unsafe conditions and the collection of time-series samples over the course of a storm hydrograph. However, autosamplers are expensive and require maintenance (for example, for intake clogging, battery and ice replacement, and programming). They also have sampling reliability issues (for example, inadvertent triggering when the stream hydrograph does not match the desired pattern, [that is, false starts], or conversely not triggering when the stream response should have dictated the desired sampling), and quality assurance concerns. As a result, although autosamplers can change the types and frequency of samples collected and make certain sample-collection schedules logistically possible, they do not necessarily reduce the expense of sampling. Finally, the use of multiple samples collected during a few storm hydrographs for regression modeling may result in serial correlation issues, artificially inflating the value of coefficients-of-determination (R^2) for regression models, and indicating a level of model robustness that may not be warranted.

Despite these issues, autosamplers can be highly useful for developing a robust dataset for refining the regression models started in this study. Primary uses for autosamplers could include

1. Unattended sampling at nights, weekends, or other situations that are difficult to sample manually;

2. Sampling in streams with rapid hydrological responses, when it may be difficult to get to the site before the peak discharge;

3. Collecting enough samples during a storm hydrograph, together with continuous monitor or streamflow data, to allow screening for key samples for laboratory submission, on the basis of peak discharge or turbidity values;

4. Collecting samples at multiple sites during a single storm, if enough autosamplers are available for deployment;

5. Collecting samples from locations that are inconvenient or unsafe for human sampling, such as manholes or culverts; and

6. Exploring within-storm variability of selected water-quality constituents, such as comparing constituent concentrations as streamflow increases and decreases during storms.

Quality assurance data collected for this study indicate that autosamplers can be used for collection of representative samples in Tualatin River basin streams, but additional tests during high streamflow conditions and at additional sites are warranted. Appropriate tests include evaluation of sample holding times, especially for bacteria and during warm weather, additional determination of cross section coefficients at high flows and at various sampling sites, and additional tests of equipment contamination or carryover when sample tubing has been deployed for extended periods.

Water Sample Collection

Historical data from USGS and Clean Water Services databases were helpful for evaluating whether or not useful regression models can be developed for Fanno Creek, Dairy Creek, and elsewhere. These databases extended the range of conditions represented in the models, increased the number of samples and thereby the degrees-of-freedom of the regressions, supported the use of several scenarios of data

aggregation to better understand the constraints of available data, and allowed validation of the developed models with independent data not used for model calibration. The historical data were collected to meet other objectives, however, and therefore were not as useful in this study for predictive purposes as might be desired. The primary limitation was the lack of samples collected during storms or other high-flow periods. Clean Water Services data were collected in a routine manner as part of an established ambient monitoring program, during which samples were sometimes collected during storm runoff, but collection was not designed specifically for those conditions. USGS data collection at Fanno Creek was mostly routine, although several additional high-flow samples had been collected as part of other studies (see Anderson and Rounds, 2003). No historical USGS data that could be used for this study were available from Dairy Creek near Highway 8. Also, USGS data did not include *E. coli* bacteria so regression models for bacteria had fewer samples to use. Additional uncertainty may have been introduced to the Fanno Creek analysis by combining analytical results from USGS and Clean Water Services databases, representing different laboratory methodologies—most likely for the suspended sediment concentration and total suspended solids data, which could not be compared because of a lack of available data from concurrent samplings.

To build on the models initiated in this report, and to develop robust regressions that can be useful for understanding concentrations and (or) loading of water-quality constituents, additional high-flow samples are needed to extend the range of conditions represented. The baseline conditions are well represented in the available data (for example, figure 3), and probably can be easily predicted. The models discussed in this report do a reasonable job of predicting a range of baseline conditions, especially for Fanno Creek, such that routine sample collection could theoretically be scaled back (regulatory considerations aside) with minimal loss of understanding of stream conditions.

Although redesigning the Clean Water Services ambient monitoring program is beyond the scope of this report, the simple addition of several samples each year from high flow conditions would allow the model results from this study to be revisited and improved upon, particularly if those samples included the most extreme conditions. If the use of surrogates for predictive modeling as outlined here were the sole objective of a modified sampling plan, at least for selected sites, it might include elements such as

1. Reducing the routine sampling frequency at each site to twice-monthly intervals, especially during low-flow periods;

2. Installing autosamplers that are designed to capture instantaneous (not flow-weighted) samples during storms, thus allowing the selection of samples for laboratory analysis (based on streamflow or turbidity, for example), and sampling during weekends and evenings, ideally with remote interrogation or activation capabilities;

3. Sampling of selected storms manually, particularly the most extreme events each year, with an added focus on collecting cross sectional data for evaluating the representativeness of the autosampler's intake location;

4. Evaluating analytical procedures, especially for *E. coli* bacteria, to ensure that resulting data will meet the needs of model development;

5. Developing predictive models for other stream constituents, such as chlorophyll, dissolved orthophosphate, or nitrogen either as total nitrogen, nitrate-nitrogen, or ammonia-nitrogen; and

6. Considering additional independent variables such as continuously monitored water temperature, optical measurements of chlorophyll or ultraviolet fluorescence, or local precipitation data.

Model Development and Selection

Log transformation of dependent variables was an important step in the development of most predictive models for this study, an approach that is similar to those from other studies. Distributions of many environmental parameters are log-normal in nature, so such transformations often are consistent with stream processes (Helsel and Hirsch, 1992). Additionally, log transformation has the practical benefit of eliminating negative results when model predictions are converted back to normal units. However, log transformation can introduce a bias that needs to be corrected. Duan's Bias Correction Factor (Duan, 1983), or BCF, which converts the logarithmic residuals from the regression process into normal space and then averages them, has been used frequently in recent studies (Uhrich and Bragg, 2003; Anderson, 2007; Rasmussen and others, 2008) and is used by the USGS as part of a national protocol for surrogate prediction by regression models (Rasmussen and others,

2009). Other steps in the maintenance of data and regression modeling include graphical evaluation of the relations between independent and dependent variables (for example, figure 5), removal of outliers (if careful attempts to resolve them were unsuccessful), and evaluation of residuals for homoscedasticity (constant variance across the range of data; Rasmussen and others, 2009).

When predicting surrogate concentrations using regression models such as those presented in this report, model uncertainty should be considered. In this study, 95 percent prediction intervals are included in figures showing time-series based on the continuously measured independent variables (for example, figure 6). For log-transformed dependent variables, lower and upper prediction interval values initially were in logarithmic terms and needed the bias correction applied after conversion to normal units in the same way as the actual predicted independent values. Although many models did not perform well for predicting the exact value of the independent variables in the validation datasets, the prediction intervals almost always encompassed the validation data. It is therefore important to display the range covered by the lower and upper prediction intervals, and equally important for water managers to consider that the actual concentration of an unmeasured constituent could fall anywhere within the portrayed interval range.

In this report, regression models were compared against an independent validation dataset through the determination of several goodness-of-fit statistics (table 8), including RMSE, a coefficient of determination analogous to the model's R^2, and the Nash-Sutcliffe coefficient, which measures the contribution of the predicted values to the measured variance. This approach appears somewhat unique among recent studies that predict surrogate values from continuous monitors, but provides a critical assessment of the model's performance against an independent dataset. The available datasets for model validation in this study were not adequate to assess model performance at the high values, most of which was during stormflow periods, so the goodness-of-fit statistics presented in this report would change if the same models were evaluated with a more complete dataset.

The use of continuous parameters such as discharge, stage, turbidity, or specific conductance for estimation of additional constituents has inherent risks of multicollinearity, wherein the independent variables are correlated, potentially causing spurious regression results or confounding the values of regression coefficients. Multicollinearity is a potential risk because many of the physical processes that affect these continuous parameters, such as discharge and turbidity, are related. Multicollinearity can be measured through the use of variance inflation factors (VIFs), which provide a measure of the independence of the individual variables, and generally is reduced with increasing numbers of samples (Draper and Smith, 1998). Assessment of multicollinearity is not straightforward, however, and must be done in conjunction with specific study objectives. In this study, VIFs were all less than general rules-of-thumb (that is, less than 5–10) that are sometimes cited (Helsel and Hirsch, 1992). Critical VIFs were calculated according to the SAS Institute's method (1989) by using the model's adjusted-R^2 in equation 3, and compared with the VIFs for the individual parameters. As a result, multicollinearity was potentially indicated for at least one or two models for each estimated parameter at each site because the respective adjusted-R^2 values were low. The collection of additional data to increase the sample size and the number of values (constituent data) measured during storm conditions would be expected to reduce the likelihood of multicollinearity among independent variables in future studies.

Model selection schemes initially used backward stepwise regression to identify potential explanatory variables, followed by the use of Mallow's Cp to reduce the likelihood of producing models that were overfitted (Helsel and Hirsch, 1992). The Best Subsets algorithm, which is widely available in many statistical software packages, makes formal use of Mallow's Cp along with alternating inclusion and exclusion of independent variables to achieve a parsimonious model (Draper and Smith, 1998). Future work on model selection also could benefit from a more broad-based selection scheme that uses all the information available from regression statistics to identify the most robust and parsimonious models, and to minimize the use of extraneous independent variables. An example model selection metric that could be useful is Akaike's Information Criterion, or AIC (Burnham and Anderson, 2002), which provides numerous scores and weights to identify the best model from a suite of potential regression models. Regardless of which of these schemes is used, however, the process can be expected to be iterative, particularly with exploration of transformation schemes and evaluation of seasonal variation by using sine and cosine transformations, while concurrently watching for potential problems with multicollinearity and serial correlation.

Conclusion

For the water-quality constituents in the small Tualatin River basin streams presented in this report, automatic samplers were capable of collecting unbiased and representative stream samples. No major cross-contamination issues from sample to sample were observed. Sufficient care certainly must be exercised to keep the samples on ice and deliver them to the laboratory in a timely manner, but when used with a good quality assurance plan, autosamplers were a useful component of a sampling plan. Used in conjunction with water-quality monitors that can trigger sampling, autosamplers may become an invaluable component of future monitoring or sampling schemes.

The use of continuously measured field parameters to predict constituents of regulatory interest in streams could be helpful for understanding the effect of management strategies on water quality in the Tualatin River basin. Results of this study indicate that the potential to develop predictive relations is good. Additional data, including more water-quality data over a broader range of conditions along with co-located discharge monitoring, would increase the predictive ability of the resulting regressions.

These sorts of predictive regression equations may be used to quantify peak concentrations or annual loads of sediment or phosphorus moving through the system. The equations may be useful in suggesting certain types of occurrences during storms or other conditions that merit further study, thus aiding in our understanding of the water-quality dynamics of these streams. This method of using continuous water-quality monitors to predict the concentrations of unmeasured water-quality constituents is an underutilized technique that deserves more attention in the future.

This study was a reconnaissance effort to determine the transferability of techniques used elsewhere to tributaries of the Tualatin River basin. These techniques for predicting the unmeasured concentrations of selected water quality constituents from continuously monitored surrogates require site-specific correlations and relatively consistent upstream conditions. If successful, this effort could provide a foundation for development of more detailed and accurate correlations at the study locations and elsewhere, and for their use in near-real time, potentially allowing evaluation of the efficacy of land-use and other management decisions.

Acknowledgments

Micelis Doyle, Anna Buckley, and Amy Brooks (USGS) all helped with data collection during this study. Two individuals volunteered their time: Steve Eikenas helped by checking on the samplers and reporting on their response to storms, and Mary Lindenberg spent many hours consolidating and making sense of the many data sources. Special thanks go to Jan Miller and the staff at the Clean Water Services Water-Quality Laboratory for their willingness to accept extra water samples and work long hours to ensure that those samples were properly analyzed.

References Cited

American Public Health Association, 1992, Standard methods for the examination of water and wastewater (18th ed.): Washington, D.C., American Public Health Association.

Anderson, C.W., 2004, Turbidity (version 2.0): U. S. Geological Survey Techniques of Water Resources Investigations, book 9, chap. A6, section 6.7, 64 p., accessed July 1, 2009, at http://water.usgs.gov/owq/FieldManual/Chapter6/6.7_contents.html.

Anderson, C.W., 2007, Influence of Cougar Reservoir drawdown on sediment and DDT transport and deposition in the McKenzie River basin, Oregon, water years 2002–04: U.S. Geological Survey Scientific-Investigations Report 2007-5164, 42 p., accessed July 1, 2009 at http://pubs.usgs.gov/sir/2007/5164/.

Anderson, C.W., and Rounds, S.A., 2003, Phosphorus and *E. coli* and their relation to selected constituents during storm runoff conditions in Fanno Creek, Oregon, 1998–99: U.S. Geological Survey Water-Resources Investigations Report 02-4232, 34 p., accessed July 1, 2009, at http://pubs.usgs.gov/wri/wri024232/pdf/wri024232.pdf.

Bonn, B.A., 1999, Selected elements and organic chemicals in bed sediment and fish tissue of the Tualatin River basin, Oregon, 1992–96: U.S. Geological Survey Water-Resources Investigations Report 99-4107, 61 p.

Bragg, H.M., Sobieszczyk, Steven, Uhrich, M.A., and Piatt, D.R., 2007, Suspended-sediment loads and yields in the North Santiam River basin, Oregon, water years 1999–2004: U.S. Geological Survey Scientific-Investigations Report 2007-5187, 26 p., accessed July 1, 2009, at http://pubs.usgs.gov/sir/2007/5187/.

Burnham, K.R., and Anderson, D.R., 2002, Model selection and multimodel interference—A practical information-theoretic approach (2d ed.): New York, Springer, 488 p.

Christensen, V.G., Jian, Xiaodong, and Ziegler, A.C., 2000, Regression analysis and real-time water-quality monitoring to estimate constituent concentrations, loads, and yields in the Little Arkansas River, south-central Kansas, 1995–99: U.S. Geological Survey Water-Resources Investigations Report 00-4126, 36 p., accessed July 1, 2009, at http://ks.water.usgs.gov/pubs/reports/wrir.00-4126_html.

Draper, N.R., and Smith, H., 1998, Applied regression analysis (3d ed.): New York, John Wiley & Sons, Ltd., 706 p.

Duan, N., 1983, Smearing estimate—A nonparametric retransformation method: Journal of the American Statistical Association, v. 78, p. 605–610.

Edwards, T.K., and Glysson, G.D., 1999, Field methods for measurement of fluvial sediment: U.S. Geological Survey Techniques of Water-Resources Investigations, book 3, chap. C2, 89 p., accessed July 1, 2009, at http://water.usgs.gov/pubs/twri/twri3-c2/.

Gray, J.R., and Glysson, G.D., eds., 2003, Proceedings of the Federal Interagency Workshop on turbidity and other sediment surrogates, April 30–May 2, 2002, Reno, Nevada: U.S. Geological Survey Circular 1250, 56 p., accessed July 1, 2009, at http://pubs.usgs.gov/circ/2003/circ1250/.

Gray, J.R., Glysson, G.D., Turcios, L.M., and Schwarz, G.E., 2000, Comparability of suspended-sediment concentration and total suspended solids data: U.S. Geological Survey Water-Resources Investigations Report 00-4191, 20 p., accessed July 1, 2009, at http://water.usgs.gov/pubs/wri/wri004191/.

Helsel, D.R., and Hirsch, R.B., 1992, Statistical methods in water resources: Amsterdam, Elsevier, 522 p.

Horowitz, A.J., Demas, C.R., Fitzgerald, K.K., Miller, T.M., and Rickert, D.A., 1994, U.S. Geological Survey protocol for the collection and processing of surface-water samples for the subsequent determination of inorganic substances in filtered water: U.S. Geological Survey Open-File Report 94-539, 57 p.

Kelly, V.J., 1997, Dissolved oxygen in the Tualatin River, Oregon, during winter conditions, 1991 and 1992: U.S. Geological Survey Water-Supply Paper 2465-A, 68 p.

Kelly, V.J., Lynch, D.D., and Rounds, S.A., 1999, Sources and transport of phosphorus and nitrogen during low-flow conditions in the Tualatin River, Oregon, 1991–1993: U.S. Geological Survey Water-Supply Paper 2465-C, 94 p.

Laenen, A., 1985, Acoustic velocity meter systems: U.S. Geological Survey Techniques of Water-Resources Investigations, book 3, chap. A17, 38 p.

Lewis, J., 1996, Turbidity-controlled suspended sediment sampling for runoff-event load estimation: Water Resources Research, v. 32, no. 7, p. 2299–2310.

Lietz, A.C., and Debiak, E.A., 2005, Development of rating curve estimators for suspended-sediment concentration and transport in the C-51 canal based on surrogate technology, Palm Beach County, Florida, 2004–05: U.S. Geological Survey Open-File Report 2005-1394, 19 p., accessed July 9, 2009, at http://pubs.usgs.gov/of/2005/1394/.

McCarthy, K.M., 2000, Phosphorus and *E. coli* in the Fanno and Bronson Creek subbasins of the Tualatin River basin, Oregon, during summer low-flow conditions, 1996: U.S. Geological Survey Water-Resources Investigations Report 00-4062, 31 p.

Nash, J.E., and Sutcliffe, J.V., 1970, River flow forecasting through conceptual models part I—A discussion of principles: Journal of Hydrology, v. 10, no. 3, p. 282–290.

Oregon Department of Environmental Quality, 1997, Oregon Administrative Rules—Dissolved oxygen standard for the Tualatin River, OAR 340–041–0445(2aE); pH standard for the Tualatin River, OAR 340–041–0445(2dB); nuisance phytoplankton growth, OAR 340–041–0150(1b); TMDLs for the Tualatin River, OAR 340–041–0470(9); policies and guidelines generally applicable to all basins, OAR 340–041–0026(3aCiii): Portland, Oreg., Department of Environmental Quality [variously paged].

Oregon Department of Environmental Quality, 2001, Tualatin River subbasin total maximum daily load: Portland, Oreg., Department of Environmental Quality, 165 p., plus appendices, accessed November 15, 2005, at http://www.deq.state.or.us/wq/TMDLs/willamette.htm.

Patton, C.J., and Kryskalla, J.R., 2003, Methods of analysis by the U.S. Geological Survey National Water Quality Laboratory—Evaluation of alkaline persulfate digestion as an alternative to Kjeldahl digestion for determination of total and dissolved nitrogen and phosphorus in water: U.S. Geological Survey Water-Resources Investigations Report 03-4174, 33 p.

Rantz, S.E., and others, 1982, Measurement and computation of streamflow—Volume 2. Computation of discharge: U.S. Geological Survey Water Supply Paper 2175, 2 v., p. 285–631.

Rasmussen, P.P., Rasmussen, T.J., Gray, J.R., Glysson, G.D., and Ziegler, A.C., 2009, Guidelines and procedures for estimating time-series suspended-sediment concentrations and loads from in-stream turbidity-sensor and streamflow data: U.S. Geological Survey Techniques and Methods, book 3, chap. C4, 57 p.

Rasmussen, T.J., Lee, C.J., and Ziegler, A.C., 2008, Estimation of constituent concentrations, loads, and yields in streams of Johnson County, northeast Kansas, using continuous water-quality monitoring and regression models, October 2002 through December 2006: U.S. Geological Survey Scientific-Investigations Report 2008-5014, 103 p., accessed on July 1, 2009, at http://pubs.usgs.gov/sir/2008/5014/.

Rounds, S.A., and Wood, T.M., 2001, Modeling water quality in the Tualatin River, Oregon, 1991–1997: U.S. Geological Survey Water-Resources Investigations Report 01-4001, 53 p.

SAS Institute, 1989, SAS/STAT users guide, version 6: SAS Institute, 1686 p.

Stone, W.W., and Wilson, J.T., 2006, Preferential flow estimates to an agricultural tile drain with implications for glyphosate transport: Journal of Environmental Quality, v. 35, no. 5, p. 1825–1835.

Uhrich, M.A., and Bragg, H.M., 2003, Monitoring instream turbidity to estimate continuous suspended-sediment loads and yields and clay-water volumes in the Upper North Santiam River basin, Oregon, 1998–2000: U.S. Geological Survey Water-Resources Investigations Report 03-4098, 43 p., accessed July 1, 2009, at http://pubs.usgs.gov/wri/WRI03-4098/.

U.S. Department of Agriculture, 1995, 1992 National Resources Inventory: Fort Worth, Tex., Soil Conservation Service National Cartography and GIS Center, tabular digital data (on CD-ROM).

U.S. Environmental Protection Agency, 2008, Clean Water Protection Act analytical methods, approved general-purpose methods: U.S. Environmental Protection Agency, accessed October 11, 2008, at http://www.epa.gov/waterscience/methods/method/.

Wagner, R.J., Boulger, R.W., Jr., Oblinger, C.J., and Smith, B.A., 2006, Guidelines and standard procedures for continuous water-quality monitors—Station operation, record computation, and data reporting: U.S. Geological Survey Techniques and Methods 1–D3, 51 p., plus 8 attachments; accessed February 17, 2010, at http://pubs.water.usgs.gov/tm1d3.

Winterstein, T.A., 1986, Effects of nozzle orientation on sediment sampling, *in* Federal Interagency Sedimentation Conference, 4th, Las Vegas, Nev., March 24–27, 1986, Proceedings: Subcommittee on Sedimentation of the Interagency Advisory Committee on Water Data, v. 1, p. 20–28.

Appendix A. Data Tables

Table A1. Water-quality and discharge data collected during sampled storms, Fanno Creek, Oregon, June 2002 and May 2003.

[**Abbreviations:** *E. coli, Escherichia coli* bacteria; °C, degrees Celsius; µS/cm, microsiemens per centimeter; mg/L, milligram per liter; FNU, formazin nephelometric unit; ft³/s, cubic foot per second; ft, foot; C/100 mL, colonies per 100 milliliters; E, estimated; <, less than]

Date (mm-dd-yy)	Time	Temperature (°C)	Specific conductance (µS/cm)	Dissolved oxygen (mg/L)	pH	Turbidity (FNU)	Discharge (ft³/s)	Stage (ft)	Total suspended solids (mg/L)	Dissolved ammonium nitrogen (mg/L)	Total Kjeldahl nitrogen (mg/L)	Nitrate + nitrite nitrogen (mg/L)	Total phosphorus (mg/L)	Soluble reactive phosphorus (mg/L)	Dissolved chloride (mg/L)	E. coli (C/100mL)
								Storm 1								
06-17-02	14 54	16.2	245	8.4	7.6	5.7	7.1	1.86	4	E 0.01	0.31	0.53	0.13	0.08	11.8	180
	15 20	16.2	245	8.4	7.6	5.9	9.0	1.91	4	<0.01	0.28	0.52	0.13	0.08	11.7	290
	15 59	16.2	241	8.5	7.7	8.4	15.3	2.06	4	<0.01	0.38	0.52	0.16	0.08	11.3	680
	16 06	16.3	240	8.5	7.7	9.0	15.3	2.06	9	<0.01	0.34	0.52	0.15	0.08	11.4	680
	16 09	16.3	240	8.5	7.7	9.0	17.8	2.11	8	<0.01	0.38	0.51	0.15	0.08	11.3	460
	16 33	16.2	243	8.5	7.6	9.8	24.2	2.22	17	<0.01	0.39	0.52	0.17	0.08	11.4	640
	17 33	16.4	228	8.2	7.6	38.2	47.0	2.55	67	0.07	0.93	0.58	0.31	0.07	10.0	2,300
	18 33	16.7	199	8.0	7.5	78.4	48.5	2.57	101	0.06	1.0	0.48	0.37	0.07	11.6	4,100
	19 33	16.4	186	7.9	7.5	104	76.9	2.91	138	0.16	1.4	0.60	0.42	0.06	7.4	E 6,400
	20 33	16.4	132	8.1	7.4	131	94.9	3.11	175	0.10	1.3	0.47	0.47	0.05	5.9	E 6,300
	21 33	16.3	139	8.1	7.4	118	89.3	3.05	160	0.07	1.2	0.44	0.43	0.06	5.7	E 6,400
	22 33	16.3	138	8.1	7.4	113	79.5	2.94	126	0.04	1.1	0.43	0.33	0.06	5.9	E 7,800
	23 33	16.4	150	7.9	7.4	73.1	75.1	2.89	88	0.03	0.93	0.45	0.31	0.06	7.0	E 10,000
06-18-02	00 33	16.4	140	7.5	7.3	82.9	72.4	2.86	85	0.08	1.1	0.48	0.30	0.05	6.4	E 8,600
	01 33	16.2	157	7.7	7.4	68.5	67.2	2.80	84	0.03	0.93	0.47	0.30	0.06	7.9	E 7,700
	02 33	16.2	147	7.5	7.3	77.8	64.7	2.77	79	<0.01	0.94	0.48	0.30	0.05	7.6	E 9,200
	03 33	16.2	149	7.3	7.3	71.0	63.9	2.76	71	0.03	1.1	0.52	0.28	0.06	7.0	E 8,000
	04 33	16.2	138	7.3	7.3	68.9	60.6	2.72	76	0.02	0.97	0.46	0.27	0.07	6.4	E 10,000
	05 33	16.1	145	7.4	7.3	71.6	56.5	2.67	75	<0.01	0.93	0.45	0.27	0.07	7.1	E 10,000
	06 33	16.1	150	7.4	7.3	65.6	54.0	2.64	72	<0.01	0.86	0.43	0.25	0.06	7.4	E 9,900
								Storm 2								
05-04-03	13 25	11.9	162	9.7	7.3	20.8	108	3.24	25	<.01	0.43	0.68	0.11	0.03	5.1	420
	14 25	12.1	139	9.9	7.3	70.9	134	3.53	84	0.02	0.48	0.62	0.19	0.03	4.8	2,300
	15 25	12.3	110	10.1	7.2	194	127	3.45	196	0.03	1.07	0.41	0.39	0.03	3.1	4,600
	16 25	12.5	123	9.9	7.2	86.6	94.9	3.09	68	0.03	0.56	0.48	0.19	0.03	3.7	4,700
	17 25	12.6	138	9.9	7.2	35.7	78.6	2.90	31	0.03	0.41	0.57	0.12	0.03	4.4	2,000
	18 25	12.6	144	9.9	7.2	28.6	71.6	2.82	21	E 0.01	0.34	0.59	0.11	0.03	4.5	1,400
	19 25	12.7	145	9.9	7.3	23.2	63.9	2.73	17	E 0.02	0.44	0.61	0.11	0.03	4.6	1,800
	20 25	12.6	148	9.9	7.3	20.9	59.8	2.67	16	E 0.02	0.32	0.62	0.10	0.03	4.9	1,200
	23 25	12.4	153	9.6	7.3	19.8	51.6	2.57	13	<0.01	0.32	0.64	0.09	0.03	5.2	380
05-05-03	02 25	12.4	162	9.6	7.3	15.6	47.0	2.51	10	E 0.02	0.27	0.67	0.09	0.04	5.7	400
	05 25	12.4	163	9.4	7.3	13.5	41.0	2.43	10	0.03	0.33	0.69	0.08	0.04	5.4	E 180

Table A1. Water-quality and discharge data collected during sampled storms, Fanno Creek, Oregon, June 2002 and May 2003.—Continued

[Abbreviations: *E. coli*, *Escherichia coli* bacteria; °C, degrees Celsius; µS/cm, microsiemens per centimeter; mg/L, milligram per liter; FNU, formazin nephelometric unit; ft³/s, cubic foot per second; ft, foot; C/100mL, colonies per 100 milliliters; E, estimated; <, less than]

Date (mm-dd-yy)	Time	Temperature (°C)	Specific conductance (µS/cm)	Dissolved oxygen (mg/L)	pH	Turbidity (FNU)	Discharge (ft³/s)	Stage (ft)	Total suspended solids (mg/L)	Dissolved ammonium nitrogen (mg/L)	Total Kjeldahl nitrogen (mg/L)	Nitrate + nitrite nitrogen (mg/L)	Total phosphorus (mg/L)	Soluble reactive phosphorus (mg/L)	Dissolved chloride (mg/L)	*E. coli* (C/100mL)
							Storm 3									
05-07-03	00 29	11.5	186	10.0	7.4	37.7	29.8	2.27	9.0	0.02	0.31	0.74	0.09	0.04	7.1	260
05-08-03	01 29	11.3	179	10.0	7.4	24.9	66.4	2.76	37.2	0.02	0.34	0.77	0.12	0.04	6.8	350
	02 29	11.3	176	9.9	7.4	40.6	91.2	3.05	69.2	0.05	0.55	0.63	0.18	0.03	5.5	640
	03 29	10.9	154	10.1	7.4	59.8	109	3.25	78.0	0.05	0.47	0.58	0.19	0.03	5.0	2,900
	04 29	11.3	158	9.8	7.4	53.0	115	3.31	66.0	0.05	0.50	0.60	0.17	0.03	5.7	1,100
	05 29	11.1	151	9.8	7.3	55.2	118	3.35	73.0	0.05	0.51	0.58	0.19	0.03	4.9	2,000
	06 29	10.8	145	9.9	7.3	52.0	115	3.32	61.0	0.03	0.48	0.59	0.18	0.04	5.9	940
	07 29	10.7	139	9.8	7.3	75.6	108	3.24	72.0	0.03	0.56	0.59	0.20	0.04	4.4	E 1,800
	08 29	10.6	139	9.7	7.3	58.0	98.5	3.13	54.0	0.03	0.49	0.59	0.18	0.04	4.2	1,300
	09 29	10.5	131	9.8	7.2	46.5	89.3	3.03	37.0	0.03	0.43	0.56	0.14	0.03	3.9	1,400
	10 29	10.5	133	9.8	7.2	51.2	83.9	2.97	40.0	0.02	0.43	0.60	0.13	0.03	4.2	E 1,900
	11 29	10.5	134	9.8	7.3	48.9	80.3	2.92	38.0	0.03	0.41	0.58	0.13	0.04	4.2	E 1,800
	12 29	10.8	138	9.8	7.3	37.7	76.0	2.87	27.0	E 0.02	0.39	0.59	0.13	0.04	4.6	1,400
	13 29	11.0	140	9.8	7.3	35.1	69.8	2.80	23.0	E 0.01	0.38	0.58	0.11	0.04	4.6	1,000
	14 29	11.0	140	9.9	7.2	32.8	63.1	2.72	18.0	E 0.01	0.29	0.59	0.10	0.03	4.6	1,100
	15 29	11.0	141	9.9	7.2	29.7	56.5	2.63	17.0	E 0.01	0.34	0.61	0.10	0.03	4.5	900
	16 29	11.2	140	9.9	7.2	29.5	50.8	2.56	16.0	<0.01	0.36	0.60	0.10	0.03	4.3	920
	17 29	11.3	140	9.9	7.2	31.0	46.2	2.50	16.0	E 0.01	0.31	0.58	0.10	0.03	4.2	960
	18 29	11.4	142	9.9	7.2	29.4	43.3	2.46	18.0	<0.01	0.32	0.59	0.10	0.03	4.4	540
	19 29	11.4	143	9.8	7.2	29.4	41.0	2.43	15.0	E 0.01	0.34	0.59	0.12	0.03	4.4	800
	20 29	11.4	145	9.8	7.2	28.2	38.8	2.40	15.0	E 0.02	0.31	0.59	0.09	0.04	4.4	720
	21 29	11.4	146	9.8	7.2	26.1	36.6	2.37	13.0	E 0.01	0.33	0.59	0.10	0.03	4.5	680
	22 29	11.4	147	9.8	7.2	25.8	35.2	2.35	12.0	E 0.02	0.29	0.59	0.09	0.04	4.6	520
	23 29	11.4	149	9.7	7.2	21.2	33.8	2.33	7.0	E 0.02	0.30	0.59	0.09	0.04	4.7	640

Table A2. Water-quality data collected during sampled storms, Beaverton Creek at 170th, Oregon, June and December 2002.

[Level is a relative measure of stream depth, taken from a bubbler anchored to the streambed at an arbitrary datum for each deployment. **Abbreviations:** *E. coli, Escherichia coli* bacteria; °C, degrees Celsius; µS/cm, microsiemens per centimeter; mg/L, milligram per liter; FNU, formazin nephelometric unit; ft, foot; C/100mL, colonies per 100 milliliters; E, estimated; >, greater than; ND, no data]

Date (mm-dd-yy)	Time	Temperature (°C)	Specific conductance (µS/cm)	Dissolved oxygen (mg/L)	pH	Turbidity (FNU)	Autosampler bubbler level (ft)	Total suspended solids (mg/L)	Dissolved ammonium nitrogen (mg/L)	Total Kjeldahl nitrogen (mg/L)	Nitrate + nitrite nitrogen (mg/L)	Total phosphorus (mg/L)	Soluble reactive phosphorus (mg/L)	Dissolved chloride (mg/L)	*E. coli* (C/100mL)
								Storm 1							
06-28-02	15 57	18.6	216	ND	7.4	14.1	ND	10	0.05	0.51	0.49	0.18	0.09	9.6	740
	16 57	18.5	212	ND	7.5	13.5	ND	12	0.06	0.61	0.48	0.20	0.10	9.9	E 1,700
	17 57	18.2	202	ND	7.5	16.0	ND	19	0.08	0.75	0.51	0.21	0.08	9.4	E 2,600
	18 57	18.0	174	ND	7.4	29.4	ND	34	0.11	0.92	0.57	0.22	0.07	10.5	E 8,200
	19 57	17.8	136	ND	7.3	42.4	ND	57	0.11	0.99	0.62	0.24	0.08	6.5	>10,000
	20 57	17.9	134	ND	7.3	44.8	ND	65	0.09	0.99	0.59	0.27	0.09	5.9	>10,000
	21 57	17.9	130	ND	7.2	48.3	ND	73	0.09	1.03	0.53	0.28	0.08	5.7	>10,000
	22 57	17.8	124	ND	7.2	68.9	ND	71	0.09	1.02	0.55	0.29	0.09	5.5	>16,000
	23 57	17.6	118	ND	7.1	59.1	ND	71	0.08	1.03	0.55	0.31	0.09	5.2	>16,000
06-29-02	00 57	17.5	114	ND	7.1	60.2	ND	90	0.07	1.07	0.55	0.35	0.11	5.1	>16,000
	01 57	17.1	110	ND	7.1	77.5	ND	97	0.07	1.11	0.54	0.38	0.11	4.9	>16,000
	02 57	17.1	106	ND	7.0	91.3	ND	134	0.06	1.06	0.56	0.38	0.11	4.5	>16,000
	03 57	17.0	106	ND	7.0	78.2	ND	136	0.06	1.02	0.57	0.37	0.13	4.5	>16,000
	04 57	16.9	106	ND	7.0	64.5	ND	121	0.05	0.98	0.57	0.32	0.12	4.5	>10,000
	05 57	16.8	108	ND	7.0	53.5	ND	90	0.04	0.96	0.56	0.35	0.13	4.6	>10,000
	06 57	16.8	108	ND	6.9	52.1	ND	81	0.04	0.91	0.52	0.31	0.15	4.6	>10,000
	07 57	16.7	110	ND	6.9	51.0	ND	55	0.04	0.85	0.48	0.30	0.15	4.6	>10,000
	08 57	16.7	108	ND	6.9	36.2	ND	39	0.03	0.84	0.45	0.29	0.15	4.6	>16,000
	09 57	16.8	108	ND	6.9	31.7	ND	33	0.03	0.81	0.42	0.28	0.15	4.4	>10,000
	14 41	18.4	101	ND	6.9	17.9	ND	18	0.03	0.69	0.36	0.23	0.14	3.8	E 8,100
	15 49	18.7	101	ND	6.9	17.0	ND	9	0.03	0.69	0.35	0.24	0.15	3.8	E 12,000
	16 49	18.9	102	ND	6.9	16.5	ND	8	0.03	0.66	0.34	0.22	0.14	3.8	E 6,800
	17 49	19.1	102	ND	6.9	16.2	ND	10	0.02	0.65	0.33	0.21	0.14	3.8	E 6,200
	18 49	19.3	103	ND	6.9	14.5	ND	8	0.03	0.64	0.31	0.20	0.15	3.8	E 6,500
	19 49	19.4	105	ND	6.9	14.4	ND	10	0.03	0.65	0.31	0.21	0.14	3.9	5,900
	20 49	19.3	107	ND	6.9	13.4	ND	10	0.03	0.61	0.30	0.20	0.13	3.9	6,800
	21 49	19.2	110	ND	6.9	15.1	ND	10	0.03	0.62	0.30	0.22	0.14	4.1	4,900
	22 49	19.0	112	ND	6.9	13.4	ND	8	0.04	0.59	0.29	0.20	0.14	4.2	4,500
	23 37	18.8	115	ND	6.9	11.9	ND	6	0.04	0.61	0.29	0.20	0.13	4.3	4,500
	23 42	18.8	115	ND	6.9	13.2	ND	8	0.04	0.62	0.29	0.19	0.13	4.3	E 3,600
	23 54	18.8	115	ND	6.9	13.1	ND	10	0.04	0.38	0.30	0.16	0.14	4.3	E 3,300
06-30-02	00 52	18.6	118	ND	6.9	11.5	ND	6	0.04	0.32	0.29	0.16	0.14	4.4	E 2,500
	00 57	18.6	118	ND	6.9	15.5	ND	8	0.05	0.28	0.29	0.17	0.14	4.3	E 2,200
	01 00	18.6	118	ND	6.9	15.5	ND	9	0.05	E 0.67	0.29	E 0.21	0.14	4.4	E 2,200
	01 07	18.5	119	ND	6.9	11.2	ND	7	0.05	E 0.68	0.29	E 0.21	0.14	4.4	E 1,600

Table A2. Water-quality data collected during sampled storms, Beaverton Creek at 170th, Oregon, June and December 2002.—Continued

[Level is a relative measure of stream depth, taken from a bubbler anchored to the streambed at an arbitrary datum for each deployment. **Abbreviations:** E. coli, Escherichia coli bacteria; °C, degrees Celsius; µS/cm, microsiemens per centimeter; mg/L, milligram per liter; FNU, formazin nephelometric unit; ft, foot; C/100mL, colonies per 100 milliliters; E, estimated; >, greater than; ND, no data]

Date (mm-dd-yy)	Time	Temperature (°C)	Specific conductance (µS/cm)	Dissolved oxygen (mg/L)	pH	Turbidity (FNU)	Autosampler bubbler level (ft)	Total suspended solids (mg/L)	Dissolved ammonium nitrogen (mg/L)	Total Kjeldahl nitrogen (mg/L)	Nitrate + nitrite nitrogen (mg/L)	Total phosphorus (mg/L)	Soluble reactive phosphorus (mg/L)	Dissolved chloride (mg/L)	E. coli (C/100mL)
							Storm 2								
12-10-02	15 16	7.8	103	9.1	6.9	55.5	0.21	79	0.08	0.77	0.54	0.28	0.08	6.3	E 1,100
	16 16	7.8	99	8.9	6.9	63.8	0.25	85	0.08	0.75	0.54	0.30	0.09	5.8	E 1,000
	17 16	7.7	101	8.7	6.9	56.6	0.28	74	0.07	0.74	0.55	0.26	0.09	6.5	E 1,300
	18 16	7.7	102	8.5	6.8	47.6	0.28	54	0.07	0.62	0.55	0.24	0.10	6.6	E 1,100
	20 16	7.5	101	8.2	6.8	42.4	0.24	40	0.05	0.61	0.51	0.21	0.10	6.2	E 900
	21 16	7.5	100	8.1	6.8	34.7	0.23	30	0.05	0.53	0.50	0.20	0.10	6.1	E 1,200
	23 16	7.4	101	7.8	6.8	30.8	0.16	21	0.04	0.53	0.49	0.19	0.09	6.0	E 1,000
12-11-02	01 16	7.3	104	7.5	6.8	25.7	0.08	15	0.04	0.47	0.50	0.18	0.09	6.1	E 1,100
	05 16	7.2	114	7.2	6.8	22.0	-0.09	10	0.05	0.47	0.52	0.16	0.09	6.4	E 1,000
	07 16	7.2	118	7.4	6.8	20.9	-0.14	8	0.05	0.49	0.54	0.16	0.08	6.6	E 940
	10 16	7.4	123	8.8	6.9	26.8	0.05	24	0.08	0.55	0.49	0.17	0.06	7.8	E 1,100
	12 16	7.7	99	9.7	6.9	52.2	0.28	72	0.07	0.64	0.42	0.24	0.08	6.5	E 830
	13 41	7.8	91	9.4	6.8	81.9	0.49	166	0.05	0.82	0.49	0.33	0.06	5.5	E 1,000
	15 41	8.0	82	9.0	6.8	74.5	0.73	158	0.04	0.85	0.44	0.35	0.07	4.9	E 1,000
	17 41	8.2	78	8.7	6.7	70.6	0.83	116	0.04	0.67	0.42	0.28	0.08	4.5	E ,1500
	19 41	8.3	78	8.4	6.7	48.2	0.66	100	0.04	0.81	0.42	0.28	0.08	4.5	1,000
	21 41	8.4	80	8.1	6.7	36.4	0.73	60	0.03	0.58	0.44	0.24	0.09	4.6	1,900
	22 41	8.5	82	8.0	6.7	42.3	0.65	48	0.03	0.52	0.45	0.22	0.09	4.6	1,400
	23 41	8.5	83	7.8	6.7	32.7	0.65	40	0.03	0.47	0.47	0.19	0.10	4.7	E 950
12-12-02	01 41	8.7	87	7.5	6.7	27.5	0.51	29	0.03	0.48	0.49	0.21	0.10	5.0	E 750
	05 41	8.9	96	6.9	6.7	25.8	0.31	19	0.04	0.45	0.55	0.18	0.09	5.5	870
	07 41	8.8	101	6.7	6.7	23.7	0.22	12	0.04	0.45	0.57	0.16	0.10	5.6	900
	09 41	8.8	104	6.5	6.7	21.6	0.13	11	0.04	0.45	0.57	0.16	0.09	5.7	E 430
	11 41	8.9	108	6.5	6.7	18.7	0.04	11	0.04	0.42	0.57	0.14	0.10	5.8	670

Table A3. Water-quality and discharge data collected during sampled storms, Chicken Creek at Scholls-Sherwood Highway, Oregon, June 2002 and May 2003.

[Abbreviations: FNU, formazin nephelometric unit; *E. coli*, *Escherichia coli* bacteria; °C, degrees Celsius; µS/cm, microsiemens per centimeter; ft³/s, cubic foot per second; ft, foot; mg/L, milligram per liter; C/100mL, colonies per 100 milliliters; E, estimated]

Date (mm-dd-yy)	Time	Temperature (°C)	Specific conductance (µS/cm)	Dissolved oxygen (mg/L)	pH	Turbidity (FNU)	Discharge (ft³/s)	Stage (ft)	Total suspended solids (mg/L)	Dissolved ammonium nitrogen (mg/L)	Total Kjeldahl nitrogen (mg/L)	Nitrate + nitrite nitrogen (mg/L)	Total phosphorus (mg/L)	Soluble reactive phosphorus (mg/L)	Dissolved chloride (mg/L)	*E. coli* (C/100mL)
									Storm 1							
06-17-02	19 50	15.7	146	6.9	7.1	15.4	12.2	1.19	15	E 0.01	0.29	0.40	0.13	0.03	3.5	220
	19 53	15.7	146	6.9	7.1	15.5	12.2	1.19	15	E 0.02	0.33	0.40	0.13	0.04	3.5	E 400
	19 55	15.7	147	6.9	7.1	15.6	12.2	1.19	15	E 0.02	0.34	0.40	0.14	0.04	3.6	E 320
	20 50	15.7	144	6.7	7.1	17.2	12.2	1.19	15	E 0.01	0.40	0.40	0.14	0.04	3.5	460
	21 50	15.6	141	6.5	7.1	16.6	12.2	1.19	15	< 0.01	0.42	0.40	0.14	0.03	3.4	980
	22 24	15.6	141	6.6	7.1	15.8	12.2	1.19	16	< 0.01	0.34	0.40	0.14	0.04	3.4	980
	22 26	15.6	141	6.6	7.1	15.7	12.2	1.19	14	< 0.01	0.37	0.40	0.14	0.03	3.4	E 1,300
	22 30	15.6	142	6.6	7.1	15.6	12.2	1.19	14	E 0.01	0.39	0.40	0.14	0.03	3.4	900
	22 32	15.6	142	6.6	7.1	15.5	12.2	1.19	14	E 0.01	0.31	0.40	0.13	0.05	3.5	840
	22 36	15.6	142	6.6	7.1	15.4	12.2	1.19	12	E 0.01	0.34	0.40	0.13	0.04	3.4	880
	22 40	15.6	142	6.6	7.1	15.3	11.6	1.18	13	E 0.01	0.38	0.41	0.15	0.04	3.5	900
	22 42	15.6	142	6.6	7.1	15.3	11.6	1.18	11	E 0.01	0.33	0.41	0.14	0.03	3.5	1,100
	23 11	15.5	141	6.7	7.1	14.8	11.6	1.18	12	E 0.02	0.38	0.41	0.14	0.04	3.5	660
	23 14	15.5	141	6.7	7.1	14.8	11.6	1.18	13	E 0.02	0.34	0.41	0.15	0.04	3.4	860
	23 18	15.5	141	6.7	7.1	14.9	11.6	1.18	15	E 0.02	0.35	0.41	0.15	0.04	3.5	840
	23 30	15.5	141	6.7	7.1	14.9	11.0	1.17	11	E 0.02	0.30	0.41	0.13	0.04	3.5	900
	23 32	15.5	140	6.7	7.1	14.9	11.0	1.17	14	E 0.02	0.32	0.41	0.14	0.04	3.5	740
	23 34	15.5	140	6.7	7.1	14.9	11.0	1.17	14	E 0.02	0.32	0.42	0.13	0.04	3.5	820
	23 36	15.5	140	6.7	7.1	14.9	11.0	1.17	16	E 0.02	0.34	0.42	0.14	0.04	3.5	680
	23 38	15.5	140	6.7	7.1	14.9	11.0	1.17	14	E 0.02	0.32	0.42	0.13	0.03	3.5	680
06-18-02	00 01	15.5	139	6.8	7.1	15.0	11.0	1.17	10	E 0.02	0.37	0.42	0.13	0.03	3.5	740
	00 25	15.4	139	6.8	7.1	14.5	10.5	1.16	14	E 0.02	0.35	0.42	0.13	0.03	3.5	760
	00 27	15.4	139	6.8	7.1	14.5	10.5	1.16	10	0.02	0.34	0.43	0.13	0.04	3.4	900
	00 29	15.4	139	6.8	7.1	14.5	10.5	1.16	10	0.02	0.33	0.43	0.13	0.04	3.4	940
									Storm 2							
05-08-03	00 35	11.0	85	9.4	7.0	31.9	20.7	1.42	28	0.02	0.20	0.78	0.10	0.02	2.7	E 64
	01 35	10.9	84	9.5	7.0	17.5	22.2	1.45	13	0.02	0.23	0.78	0.08	0.02	2.7	180
	02 35	10.9	85	9.3	7.0	18.0	22.2	1.45	10	0.03	0.21	0.79	0.08	0.03	2.7	300
	03 35	10.8	86	9.4	7.0	13.8	23.2	1.47	11	0.03	0.21	0.76	0.08	0.03	2.7	120

Table A3. Water-quality and discharge data collected during sampled storms, Chicken Creek, Oregon, June 2002 and May 2003.—Continued

[Abbreviations: FNU, formazin nephelometric unit; *E. coli*, *Escherichia coli* bacteria; °C, degrees Celsius; µS/cm, microsiemens per centimeter; ft³/s, cubic foot per second; ft, foot; mg/L, milligram per liter; C/100mL, colonies per 100 milliliters; E, estimated]

Date (mm-dd-yy)	Time	Temperature (°C)	Specific conductance (µS/cm)	Dissolved oxygen (mg/L)	pH	Turbidity (FNU)	Discharge (ft³/s)	Stage (ft)	Total suspended solids (mg/L)	Dissolved ammonium nitrogen (mg/L)	Total Kjeldahl nitrogen (mg/L)	Nitrate + nitrite nitrogen (mg/L)	Total phosphorus (mg/L)	Soluble reactive phosphorus (mg/L)	Dissolved chloride (mg/L)	*E. coli* (C/100mL)
								Storm 3								
05-17-03	18 00	10.9	95	9.9	7.0	31.2	22.7	1.46	30	0.03	0.28	0.52	0.12	0.03	2.7	600
	19 00	10.8	94	10.0	7.0	29.2	26.8	1.54	27	0.04	0.35	0.51	0.12	0.03	2.7	E 700
	20 00	10.7	88	10.2	7.0	38.2	28.9	1.58	29	0.03	0.34	0.50	0.13	0.02	2.6	950
	21 00	10.7	93	10.2	7.0	31.3	27.8	1.56	31	0.04	0.37	0.50	0.14	0.02	2.7	3,900
	22 00	10.4	88	9.8	7.0	49.1	25.7	1.52	26	0.03	0.36	0.47	0.13	0.02	2.6	3,800
	23 00	10.2	89	10.0	6.9	31.5	23.7	1.48	22	0.03	0.34	0.49	0.13	0.03	2.7	2,200
05-18-03	00 00	10.1	92	9.8	6.9	23.0	21.2	1.43	14	0.03	0.28	0.51	0.09	0.02	2.7	1,900
	01 00	9.9	92	9.8	6.9	20.1	19.8	1.40	11	0.03	0.28	0.53	0.09	0.03	2.7	1,600
	05 00	9.2	90	10.1	6.9	19.3	17.0	1.34	9	0.03	0.23	0.55	0.08	0.02	2.6	1,200
	06 00	9.1	90	10.1	6.9	17.7	17.0	1.34	9	0.03	0.24	0.54	0.08	0.02	2.5	1,200
	11 00	9.3	92	10.4	6.9	17.1	16.5	1.33	7	0.03	0.22	0.53	0.08	0.02	2.5	940
	12 00	9.6	92	10.6	6.9	16.8	16.1	1.32	9	0.03	0.26	0.54	0.09	0.02	2.5	1,000
	13 00	10.2	92	10.4	6.9	15.3	16.1	1.32	7	0.03	0.27	0.54	0.09	0.02	2.5	740
	16 00	11.8	94	10.6	7.0	13.4	15.6	1.31	5	0.03	0.26	0.56	0.08	0.02	2.6	E 360
	17 00	12.0	95	10.4	7.0	12.4	15.6	1.31	5	0.03	0.24	0.56	0.08	0.02	2.6	540

Table A4. Water-quality and discharge data collected during sampled storms, Rock Creek at Woll Pond Way, Oregon, June and December 2002, and September 2003.

[Level is a relative measure of stream depth, taken from a bubbler anchored to the streambed at an arbitrary datum for each deployment. **Abbreviations:** FNU, formazin nephelometric unit; *E. coli, Escherichia coli* bacteria; °C, degrees Celsius; µS/cm, microsiemens per centimeter; mg/L, milligram per liter; ft, foot; ft³/s, cubic foot per second; C/100mL, colonies per 100 milliliters; E, estimated; >, greater than; ND, no data]

Date (mm-dd-yy)	Time	Temperature (°C)	Specific conductance (µS/cm)	Dissolved oxygen (mg/L)	pH	Turbidity (FNU)	Autosampler bubbler level (ft)	Discharge (ft³/s)	Total suspended solids (mg/L)	Dissolved ammonium nitrogen (mg/L)	Total Kjeldahl nitrogen (mg/L)	Nitrate + nitrite nitrogen (mg/L)	Total phosphorus (mg/L)	SRP (mg/L)	Dissolved chloride (mg/L)	E. coli (C/100mL)
								Storm 1								
06-28-02	17 12	18.3	234	6.5	7.6	15	ND	13.3	17	E 0.01	0.52	0.77	0.26	0.17	11.7	E 1,300
	17 22	18.3	236	6.5	7.6	16	ND	13.3	20	E 0.02	0.49	0.75	0.26	0.17	11.7	E 1,600
	17 27	18.2	238	6.5	7.5	16	ND	13.9	20	E 0.02	0.53	0.74	0.26	0.17	11.7	E 1,700
	18 17	18.2	240	6.4	7.5	22	ND	15.7	31	E 0.02	0.55	0.63	0.29	0.16	12.4	E 2,300
	19 17	18.1	240	6.5	7.5	28	ND	20.6	41	0.03	0.66	0.54	0.31	0.15	13.0	E 2,400
	20 17	18.0	238	6.4	7.5	37	ND	23.6	52	0.03	0.70	0.50	0.31	0.14	12.3	E 2,400
	21 17	17.9	214	6.5	7.5	48	ND	30.9	64	0.02	0.82	0.44	0.33	0.14	9.8	E 5,100
	22 17	17.8	194	6.7	7.5	51	ND	41.1	72	0.04	0.86	0.46	0.33	0.14	8.2	> 6,000
	23 17	17.8	186	6.7	7.4	53	ND	54.1	76	0.04	0.76	0.45	0.34	0.14	8.1	> 8,000
06-29-02	00 17	17.8	184	6.7	7.4	55	ND	69.3	82	0.09	0.92	0.78	0.42	0.19	8.4	> 10,000
	01 17	17.8	172	6.7	7.4	61	ND	86.6	96	0.07	0.94	0.56	0.37	0.16	7.5	> 10,000
	02 17	17.7	164	6.7	7.4	66	ND	107	103	0.04	0.91	0.42	0.36	0.14	8.3	> 10,000
	03 17	17.7	154	6.7	7.3	67	ND	128	96	0.04	0.91	0.41	0.34	0.12	6.9	> 10,000
	04 17	17.7	156	6.8	7.3	65	ND	153	95	0.04	0.87	0.41	0.35	0.12	7.3	> 10,000
	05 17	17.6	146	6.7	7.3	67	ND	172	94	0.04	0.91	0.39	0.33	0.12	7.0	> 10,000
	06 17	17.6	132	6.6	7.2	70	ND	180	96	0.04	0.92	0.40	0.33	0.11	6.1	> 10,000
	07 17	17.5	128	6.6	7.2	78	ND	181	95	0.04	0.91	0.40	0.33	0.12	5.8	> 7,500
	15 55	18.0	136	6.4	7.1	45	ND	130	61	0.04	0.76	0.54	0.27	0.13	7.4	4,600
	16 55	18.1	138	6.4	7.1	42	ND	124	49	0.04	0.86	0.50	0.26	0.12	7.4	4,400
	17 55	18.2	138	6.4	7.1	41	ND	118	48	0.03	0.73	0.43	0.24	0.13	7.4	5,400
	18 55	18.3	138	6.4	7.2	38	ND	112	43	0.03	0.73	0.40	0.25	0.13	7.3	3,900
	19 55	18.4	138	6.4	7.2	39	ND	107	53	0.03	0.74	0.38	0.25	0.13	7.3	4,800
	20 55	18.6	138	6.4	7.2	35	ND	103	39	0.03	0.65	0.37	0.25	0.13	7.3	4,700
	21 55	19.6	138	6.4	7.2	31	ND	98.9	37	0.03	0.61	0.35	0.23	0.13	7.2	4,600
	22 55	18.7	138	6.3	7.2	29	ND	94.0	33	0.03	0.65	0.34	0.22	0.13	7.1	3,400
	23 55	18.7	138	6.3	7.2	28	ND	65.1	31	0.03	0.55	0.34	0.22	0.13	7.1	3,300
06-30-02	00 55	18.6	138	6.3	7.2	27	ND	85.1	33	0.03	0.64	0.33	0.22	0.14	7.3	2,200
	01 55	18.5	140	6.3	7.2	26	ND	80.1	29	0.04	0.58	0.33	0.21	0.14	7.2	2,400
	02 55	18.5	140	6.3	7.2	25	ND	75.9	30	0.03	0.55	0.32	0.21	0.14	7.2	1,600
	03 55	18.4	140	6.3	7.2	22	ND	71.8	29	0.07	0.80	0.33	0.26	0.17	7.3	2,200
	04 55	18.3	142	6.3	7.2	22	ND	67.9	21	0.03	0.59	0.31	0.21	0.13	7.3	E 2,100
	05 55	18.3	142	6.3	7.2	23	ND	64.0	25	0.04	0.60	0.31	0.21	0.13	7.4	E 2,200

Table A4. Water-quality and discharge data collected during sampled storms, Rock Creek at Woll Pond Way, Oregon, June and December 2002, and September 2003.—Continued

[Level is a relative measure of stream depth, taken from a bubbler anchored to the streambed at an arbitrary datum for each deployment. **Abbreviations:** FNU, formazin nephelometric unit; *E. coli, Escherichia coli* bacteria; °C, degrees Celsius; μS/cm, microsiemens per centimeter; mg/L, milligram per liter; ft, foot; ft³/s, cubic foot per second; C/100mL, colonies per 100 milliliters; E, estimated; >, greater than; ND, no data]

Date (mm-dd-yy)	Time	Temperature (°C)	Specific conductance (μS/cm)	Dissolved oxygen (mg/L)	pH	Turbidity (FNU)	Autosampler bubbler level (ft)	Discharge (ft³/s)	Total suspended solids (mg/L)	Dissolved ammonium nitrogen (mg/L)	Total Kjeldahl nitrogen (mg/L)	Nitrate + nitrite nitrogen (mg/L)	Total phosphorus (mg/L)	SRP (mg/L)	Dissolved chloride (mg/L)	E. coli (C/100mL)
							Storm 2									
12-10-02	14 56	6.3	167	10.5	7.3	78	0.57	151	106	0.10	1.0	0.49	0.32	0.08	11.6	E 700
	15 56	6.6	155	10.3	7.3	81	0.67	180	99	0.10	0.86	0.49	0.31	0.08	12.2	2,200
	16 56	6.8	134	10.4	7.3	77	0.69	184	98	0.10	0.87	0.47	0.31	0.10	9.7	E 1,600
	17 56	6.9	129	10.4	7.2	71	0.67	180	90	0.09	0.82	0.46	0.29	0.08	9.3	E 1,600
	18 56	6.9	131	10.3	7.2	69	0.64	175	77	0.09	0.77	0.49	0.30	0.09	9.8	E 1,900
	19 56	6.9	129	10.4	7.2	60	0.59	171	66	0.09	0.73	0.47	0.26	0.09	10.0	E 700
	20 56	6.9	131	10.3	7.2	54	0.55	168	62	0.08	0.71	0.49	0.25	0.10	9.9	E 1,500
	21 56	6.9	134	10.3	7.2	48	0.48	164	55	0.08	0.70	0.49	0.23	0.09	10.1	E 900
	22 56	6.9	133	10.3	7.2	47	0.41	161	51	0.07	0.66	0.47	0.24	0.09	10.4	E 1,100
	23 56	7.0	132	10.4	7.2	46	0.32	156	49	0.07	0.66	0.47	0.21	0.09	11.6	E 1,400
12-11-02	11 15	6.9	139	10.5	7.1	36	0.28	93	36	0.05	0.54	0.41	0.20	0.08	12.8	E 900
	12 15	6.9	140	10.7	7.1	50	0.84	106	59	0.05	0.62	0.40	0.22	0.08	12.9	E 700
	13 15	7.1	132	10.7	7.1	59	1.33	143	73	0.06	0.67	0.41	0.24	0.09	11.7	E 1,800
	14 15	7.2	124	10.7	7.1	62	1.69	197	96	0.06	0.65	0.40	0.26	0.09	10.7	2,100
	15 16	7.3	115	10.8	7.1	66	1.89	241	88	0.05	0.65	0.37	0.26	0.09	9.7	1,600
	17 16	7.4	100	10.7	7.0	71	2.07	287	93	0.05	0.65	0.37	0.25	0.09	8.0	1,400
	19 16	7.6	105	10.5	7.0	72	2.06	287	82	0.04	0.68	0.39	0.27	0.09	8.9	E 950
	21 16	7.7	108	10.5	7.0	67	1.98	275	73	0.04	0.69	0.43	0.27	0.09	9.5	1,600
	23 16	7.8	109	10.5	7.0	66	1.81	260	73	0.04	0.69	0.47	0.25	0.08	9.5	1,600
12-12-02	02 16	8.0	109	10.2	6.9	55	1.50	337	58	0.04	0.63	0.45	0.22	0.09	9.5	1,000
	03 16	8.0	109	10.2	6.9	53	1.38	355	56	0.04	0.60	0.44	0.22	0.08	9.4	E 950
	05 16	8.1	109	10.1	6.9	47	1.07	372	43	0.04	0.55	0.46	0.22	0.08	9.3	1,300
	07 16	8.2	109	10.1	6.9	44	0.73	370	39	0.03	0.55	0.47	0.19	0.08	9.0	E 550
	09 16	8.3	112	10.1	6.9	36	0.41	363	34	0.03	0.44	0.48	0.17	0.08	9.3	1200
	11 16	8.3	116	10.0	6.9	31	0.11	344	25	0.03	0.46	0.48	0.17	0.09	9.9	E 700
	13 16	8.4	119	10.0	6.9	27	-0.18	317	21	0.03	0.44	0.49	0.16	0.08	10.5	E 450

Table A4. Water-quality and discharge data collected during sampled storms, Rock Creek at Woll Pond Way, Oregon, June and December 2002, and September 2003.—Continued

[Level is a relative measure of stream depth, taken from a bubbler anchored to the streambed at an arbitrary datum for each deployment. **Abbreviations:** FNU, formazin nephelometric unit; *E. coli*, *Escherichia coli* bacteria; °C, degrees Celsius; µS/cm, microsiemens per centimeter; mg/L, milligram per liter; ft, foot; ft³/s, cubic foot per second; C/100mL, colonies per 100 milliliters; E, estimated; >, greater than; ND, no data]

Date (mm-dd-yy)	Time	Temperature (°C)	Specific conductance (µS/cm)	Dissolved oxygen (mg/L)	pH	Turbidity (FNU)	Autosampler bubbler level (ft)	Discharge (ft³/s)	Total suspended solids (mg/L)	Dissolved ammonium nitrogen (mg/L)	Total Kjeldahl nitrogen (mg/L)	Nitrate + nitrite nitrogen (mg/L)	Total phosphorus (mg/L)	SRP (mg/L)	Dissolved chloride (mg/L)	E. coli (C/100mL)
								Storm 3								
09-07-03	02 05	19.2	290	5.8	7.6	26	ND	5.24	4.0	0.03	0.37	0.50	0.25	0.19	23.1	E 100
	03 05	19.0	289	5.8	7.6	20	ND	5.24	5.0	0.03	0.32	0.50	0.23	0.19	22.8	E 100
	05 05	18.7	287	5.8	7.6	28	ND	5.24	5.0	0.02	0.36	0.55	0.24	0.19	21.9	>120
	08 05	18.5	284	5.9	7.6	33	ND	5.76	4.0	0.02	0.32	0.69	0.23	0.19	20.8	E 84
	11 05	18.7	282	6.2	7.6	32	ND	5.68	4.0	0.03	0.36	0.58	0.25	0.20	20.1	E 120
	13 05	18.9	281	6.3	7.6	33	ND	5.54	4.0	0.03	0.31	0.55	0.23	0.20	19.9	E 84
	16 05	19.1	281	6.2	7.6	30	ND	5.81	5.0	0.03	0.26	0.55	0.23	0.19	19.3	E 67
	17 05	19.1	280	6.1	7.6	36	ND	6.03	3.0	0.03	0.32	0.55	0.25	0.20	19.1	>100
	18 05	19.0	277	6.2	7.6	43	ND	6.16	21.0	0.02	0.41	0.56	0.27	0.20	18.6	1100
	19 05	18.9	277	6.1	7.6	44	ND	6.25	8.0	E 0.02	0.36	0.55	0.25	0.20	18.3	620
	20 05	18.8	274	6.0	7.6	45	ND	6.41	8.0	0.07	0.56	0.55	0.26	0.20	17.6	550
	21 05	18.7	243	5.9	7.6	56	ND	6.55	13.0	0.10	0.61	0.51	0.25	0.19	15.5	650
	22 05	18.5	262	5.9	7.6	59	ND	6.83	16.0	0.04	0.52	0.50	0.28	0.20	16.8	620
	23 05	18.3	262	5.8	7.6	54	ND	7.20	12.0	0.05	0.50	0.52	0.25	0.20	16.2	630
09-08-03	00 05	18.0	250	6.0	7.6	60	ND	8.10	9.0	0.05	0.53	0.54	0.25	0.19	15.2	780
	18 30	17.8	246	6.2	7.6	79	ND	25.4	13.0	0.05	0.60	0.49	0.21	0.14	14.0	E 600
	19 30	17.7	243	6.0	7.4	79	ND	24.8	12.0	0.05	0.62	0.55	0.18	0.13	14.0	E 1,000
	20 30	17.6	239	5.7	7.4	73	ND	23.9	15.5	0.06	0.84	0.61	0.20	0.14	14.1	E 1,000
	21 30	17.6	236	5.6	7.4	71	ND	23.2	18.5	0.07	0.84	0.67	0.21	0.13	14.1	E 2,200
	22 30	17.5	233	5.4	7.4	81	ND	22.5	24.5	0.07	0.92	0.72	0.22	0.13	14.1	E 1,400
	23 30	17.5	229	5.3	7.3	77	ND	21.8	25.0	0.08	0.95	0.75	0.21	0.12	13.7	>3,600
09-09-03	00 30	17.5	222	5.4	7.3	79	ND	22.6	24.5	0.08	0.90	0.65	0.22	0.12	13.5	E 1,600
	01 30	17.5	222	5.6	7.3	81	ND	25.8	24.0	0.07	0.85	0.57	0.21	0.12	14.1	E 2,000
	02 30	17.5	216	5.7	7.3	82	ND	30.1	21.0	0.07	0.86	0.55	0.20	0.12	13.7	E 2,400
	03 30	17.4	208	5.7	7.3	78	ND	31.1	20.0	0.07	1.10	0.54	0.23	0.12	13.1	E 2,000
	04 30	17.2	206	5.8	7.3	82	ND	31.1	22.0	0.06	1.10	0.55	0.21	0.13	12.8	E 600
	05 30	17.0	219	6.0	7.3	83	ND	29.6	33.0	0.06	0.86	0.57	0.25	0.14	12.0	E 1,000
	06 30	16.6	210	6.2	7.4	90	ND	28.0	60.0	0.06	0.90	0.45	0.27	0.13	10.2	E 2,800
	07 30	16.5	209	6.0	7.3	85	ND	27.2	70.0	0.05	1.00	0.46	0.30	0.13	10.3	E 3,600
	08 30	16.4	191	6.2	7.3	106	ND	29.3	110.0	0.05	1.10	0.42	0.37	0.12	9.2	8,400
	09 30	16.4	183	6.4	7.3	99	ND	34.2	113.0	0.06	1.10	0.40	0.33	0.12	9.4	5,600
	10 30	16.3	162	6.6	7.2	99	ND	42.8	109.0	0.09	1.20	0.39	0.34	0.12	8.1	12,000
	11 30	16.4	155	6.6	7.2	99	ND	53.1	112.0	0.10	0.98	0.50	0.35	0.13	8.0	12,000
	12 30	16.4	143	6.8	7.2	103	ND	70.7	112.0	0.09	0.92	0.45	0.33	0.13	7.3	11,000

Table A5. Water-quality and discharge data collected during sampled storms, Dairy Creek at Highway 8, Oregon, October and November 2003.

[**Abbreviations:** FNU, formazin nephelometric unit; *E. coli, Escherichia coli* bacteria; °C, degrees Celsius; µS/cm, microsiemens per centimeter; mg/L, milligram per liter; ft³/s, cubic foot per second; ft, foot; C/100mL, colonies per 100 milliliters; E, estimated; <, less than]

Date (mm-dd-yy)	Time	Temperature (°C)	Specific conductance (µS/cm)	Dissolved oxygen (mg/L)	pH	Turbidity (FNU)	Discharge (ft³/s)	Stage (ft)	Total suspended solids (mg/L)	Dissolved ammonium nitrogen (mg/L)	Total Kjeldahl nitrogen (mg/L)	Nitrate + nitrite nitrogen (mg/L)	Total phosphorus (mg/L)	Soluble reactive phosphorus (mg/L)	Dissolved chloride (mg/L)	E. coli (C/100mL)
							Storm 1									
10-09-03	01 25	14.2	140	7.4	7.6	5.8	39.1	3.2	7	0.03	0.41	0.45	0.14	0.07	5.14	E 45
	02 25	14.1	140	7.5	7.6	7.5	39.1	3.2	7	0.03	0.36	0.45	0.14	0.07	5.12	E 95
	03 25	14.0	140	7.5	7.6	5.7	39.1	3.2	5	0.03	0.39	0.45	0.14	0.07	5.11	E 65
	04 25	13.9	139	7.5	7.6	6.1	38.8	3.2	8	0.03	0.36	0.45	0.13	0.07	5.19	E 40
	05 25	13.9	139	7.6	7.6	6.7	38.8	3.2	7	0.03	0.38	0.46	0.14	0.07	5.16	E 85
	06 25	13.8	139	7.6	7.6	6.5	38.8	3.2	8	0.03	0.37	0.46	0.14	0.07	4.89	E 60
	07 25	13.7	141	7.6	7.6	6.4	38.7	3.2	9	0.03	0.38	0.48	0.14	0.07	5.14	E 60
	08 25	13.6	140	7.6	7.6	6.5	39.1	3.2	7	0.03	0.38	0.52	0.14	0.07	5.10	E 85
							Storm 2									
11-19-03	00 45	8.9	122	3.2	7.3	27.3	74.1	4.0	8	0.03	0.37	0.23	0.09	0.04	5.33	140
	01 45	9.0	122	3.1	7.3	10.0	73.0	4.0	8	0.02	0.34	0.23	0.09	0.04	5.34	160
	02 45	9.0	122	3.1	7.3	9.0	72.5	4.0	8	0.02	0.37	0.23	0.10	0.04	5.29	230
	03 45	9.0	122	3.0	7.3	9.0	72.5	4.0	6	E 0.02	0.37	0.23	0.09	0.04	5.29	160
	04 45	9.1	122	2.9	7.3	8.8	74.6	4.0	8	0.02	0.36	0.23	0.09	0.04	5.23	170
	05 45	9.1	122	2.9	7.3	9.1	76.7	4.1	9	E 0.02	0.38	0.23	0.10	0.04	5.26	320
	06 45	9.1	122	2.8	7.3	9.8	75.6	4.1	10	E 0.01	0.38	0.24	0.10	0.04	5.20	E 400
	07 45	9.1	120	2.8	7.3	11.5	76.1	4.1	11	E 0.01	0.38	0.24	0.11	0.05	5.01	340
	08 45	9.0	117	2.7	7.3	14.2	79.3	4.1	12	E 0.01	0.36	0.26	0.11	0.04	5.00	330
	09 45	8.9	124	2.6	7.3	10.8	84.8	4.2	12	E 0.01	0.34	0.26	0.11	0.04	5.35	220
	10 45	8.9	125	2.6	7.3	13.4	90.6	4.3	11	E 0.01	0.38	0.26	0.11	0.05	5.38	280
	11 45	8.8	126	2.5	7.3	15.0	94.2	4.4	10	E 0.01	0.37	0.27	0.12	0.05	5.45	520
	12 45	8.7	126	2.5	7.3	14.9	99.1	4.5	16	E 0.01	0.41	0.37	0.14	0.07	5.19	E 380
	13 45	8.7	123	2.4	7.3	19.5	106.0	4.6	19	E 0.01	0.41	0.44	0.17	0.09	5.03	900
	14 45	8.8	125	2.3	7.3	21.4	113.3	4.7	27	E 0.02	0.48	0.40	0.19	0.09	5.16	750
	15 45	8.7	124	2.3	7.3	26.9	113.3	4.7	31	E 0.02	0.48	0.41	0.19	0.09	5.11	950
	16 26	8.6	123	2.7	7.3	30.1	120.1	4.8	29	< 0.01	0.47	0.43	0.21	0.10	5.46	E 520
	17 26	8.6	123	5.9	7.3	21.6	121.7	4.8	25	< 0.01	0.51	0.46	0.23	E 0.10	5.48	780
	18 26	8.6	124	5.4	7.3	23.9	121.4	4.8	20	< 0.01	0.53	0.50	0.22	0.10	5.69	760
	19 26	8.6	125	6.0	7.4	23.4	121.2	4.8	21	< 0.01	0.53	0.52	0.21	0.10	5.63	720
	20 26	8.5	124	5.9	7.4	21.8	120.3	4.8	22	E 0.01	0.45	0.48	0.20	0.09	5.67	640
	21 26	8.5	123	5.6	7.3	20.1	117.7	4.8	16	< 0.01	0.44	0.47	0.16	0.08	5.68	480
	22 26	8.4	123	6.0	7.3	17.0	115.6	4.7	15	< 0.01	0.41	0.46	0.16	0.08	5.60	E 360
11-20-03	00 26	8.3	123	6.0	7.3	15.0	112.7	4.7	13	< 0.01	0.43	0.44	0.14	0.07	5.59	250
	02 26	8.2	126	6.0	7.3	14.5	112.7	4.7	11	< 0.01	0.44	0.45	0.14	0.06	5.78	290
	04 26	8.1	132	6.5	7.3	18.4	116.6	4.7	16	E 0.01	0.40	0.49	0.14	0.06	6.02	270
	06 26	8.0	132	5.4	7.3	16.3	125.6	4.9	14	E 0.01	0.44	0.49	0.15	0.06	6.21	200
	08 26	7.9	132	4.9	7.3	15.7	138.3	5.0	12	E 0.01	0.37	0.53	0.15	0.05	6.22	180
	10 26	7.9	133	4.6	7.3	15.6	152.6	5.2	15	E 0.01	0.34	0.64	0.14	0.05	6.04	160
	11 26	7.9	135	4.3	7.3	15.1	158.7	5.3	13	E 0.02	0.48	0.70	0.14	0.05	6.42	190

Table A6. Water-quality and discharge data collected during sampled storm, Gales Creek at Old Highway 47, Oregon, November 2003.

[Abbreviations: FNU, formazin nephelometric unit; *E. coli*, *Escherichia coli* bacteria; °C, degrees Celsius; µS/cm, microsiemens per centimeter; mg/L, milligram per liter; ft³/s, cubic foot per second; ft, foot; C/100mL, colonies per 100 milliliters; E, estimated; <, less than]

Date (mm-dd-yy)	Time	Temperature (°C)	Specific conductance (µS/cm)	Dissolved oxygen (mg/L)	pH	Turbidity (FNU)	Discharge (ft³/s)	Stage (ft)	Total suspended solids (mg/L)	Dissolved ammonium nitrogen (mg/L)	Total Kjeldahl nitrogen (mg/L)	Nitrate + nitrite nitrogen (mg/L)	Total phosphorus (mg/L)	Soluble reactive phosphorus (mg/L)	Dissolved chloride (mg/L)	*E. coli* (C/100mL)
							Storm 1									
11-17-03	15 04	7.9	99	11.3	7.5	24.3	180.40	3.30	24	<0.01	0.31	0.47	0.06	0.02	5.09	560
	16 04	7.9	99	11.3	7.5	18.1	180.91	3.31	46	<0.01	0.29	0.47	0.07	0.02	5.05	600
	17 04	8.0	99	11.3	7.5	18.3	179.51	3.29	45	<0.01	0.33	0.49	0.08	0.02	5.11	220
	18 04	8.1	99	11.3	7.5	13.8	176.61	3.25	41	<0.01	0.28	0.50	0.06	0.02	5.03	240
	19 04	8.2	99	11.3	7.5	17.5	173.71	3.21	38	<0.01	0.28	0.50	0.06	0.01	5.15	280
	20 04	8.2	98	11.3	7.5	14.1	170.91	3.17	34	<0.01	0.28	0.50	0.06	0.01	5.21	420
	21 04	8.3	97	11.3	7.5	13.9	168.01	3.13	26	E 0.01	0.27	0.51	0.05	0.02	5.21	210
	22 04	8.4	97	11.2	7.5	11.3	165.91	3.10	18	<0.01	0.21	0.51	E 0.05	0.02	5.18	190
	23 04	8.5	98	11.2	7.5	10.8	163.90	3.07	20	<0.01	0.22	0.51	E 0.04	0.02	5.20	190
11-18-03	00 04	8.6	97	11.1	7.5	10.7	163.20	3.06	20	<0.01	0.24	0.51	E 0.05	0.02	5.22	200
	03 04	8.7	98	11.0	7.5	12.0	161.10	3.03	15	<0.01	0.21	0.51	E 0.04	0.01	5.15	120
	04 04	8.7	98	11.0	7.5	10.8	161.10	3.03	16	<0.01	0.2	0.52	E 0.05	0.02	4.96	110
	05 04	8.8	98	10.9	7.5	11.3	162.50	3.05	16	<0.01	0.22	0.57	E 0.05	0.02	5.12	110
	06 04	8.8	98	10.9	7.5	12.4	163.39	3.06	15	<0.01	0.2	0.54	E 0.04	0.02	5.12	180
	07 04	8.8	98	10.9	7.5	12.3	163.90	3.07	18	<0.01	0.2	0.54	E 0.04	0.01	5.20	200
	08 04	8.9	98	10.9	7.5	9.0	164.89	3.08	18	<0.01	0.21	0.56	E 0.04	0.02	5.18	150
	11 04	9.1	99	10.9	7.5	9.8	168.20	3.13	14	<0.01	0.2	0.6	E 0.04	0.02	5.15	E 130
	12 10	9.3	100	10.9	7.5	37.5	168.90	3.14	12	<0.01	0.18	0.63	E 0.04	0.02	4.87	120
	13 10	9.3	101	10.8	7.5	15.7	168.90	3.14	14	E 0.01	0.19	0.67	E 0.05	0.02	4.70	140
	14 10	9.4	101	10.8	7.5	11.7	169.60	3.15	15	<0.01	0.19	0.71	E 0.04	0.02	4.90	140
	15 10	9.5	101	10.8	7.5	10.4	170.40	3.16	14	<0.01	0.2	0.65	E 0.05	0.02	4.84	100
	18 10	9.7	100	10.8	7.5	18.8	170.40	3.16	18	<0.01	0.17	0.66	0.05	0.02	4.75	120
	20 10	9.9	98	10.8	7.5	10.6	168.20	3.13	17	<0.01	0.18	0.66	E 0.04	0.02	4.63	E 95
11-19-03	03 10	10.3	96	10.5	7.5	8.1	162.50	3.05	10	<0.01	0.17	0.56	E 0.04	0.02	4.12	320
	04 10	10.3	95	10.4	7.5	15.8	162.27	3.05	14	<0.01	0.18	0.60	E 0.05	0.02	4.15	E 1,200
	05 10	10.3	95	10.4	7.5	40.0	163.20	3.06	13	E 0.01	0.17	0.54	E 0.04	0.02	4.09	290
	06 10	10.2	95	10.4	7.5	[1]150.5	164.43	3.08	9	<0.01	0.17	0.57	0.05	0.02	4.15	100
	07 10	10.2	95	10.4	7.5	9.4	165.87	3.10	15	<0.01	0.18	0.55	0.05	0.02	4.25	160
	08 10	10.1	95	10.4	7.5	13.7	167.27	3.12	17	<0.01	0.18	0.52	0.05	0.02	4.64	560
	09 10	10.0	95	10.4	7.5	15.0	170.60	3.16	14	<0.01	0.17	0.52	E 0.04	0.02	4.18	530
	10 10	9.9	94	10.4	7.5	16.5	174.90	3.22	15	<0.01	0.17	0.51	E 0.05	0.02	4.02	400
	14 35	9.4	94	10.6	7.4	34.1	214.53	3.77	53	<0.01	0.23	0.54	0.08	0.02	4.61	E 100
	15 35	9.2	93	10.7	7.5	26.3	226.73	3.93	53	<0.01	0.24	0.55	0.09	0.02	4.45	E 200

Table A6. Water quality and discharge data collected during sampled storm, Gales Creek at Old Highway 47, Oregon, November 2003.—Continued

[**Abbreviations:** FNU, formazin nephelometric unit; *E. coli, Escherichia coli* bacteria; °C, degrees Celsius; µS/cm, microsiemens per centimeter; mg/L, milligram per liter; ft³/s, cubic foot per second; ft, foot; C/100mL, colonies per 100 milliliters; E, estimated; <, less than]

Date (mm-dd-yy)	Time	Temperature (°C)	Specific conductance (µS/cm)	Dissolved oxygen (mg/L)	pH	Turbidity (FNU)	Discharge (ft³/s)	Stage (ft)	Total suspended solids (mg/L)	Dissolved ammonium nitrogen (mg/L)	Total Kjeldahl nitrogen (mg/L)	Nitrate + nitrite nitrogen (mg/L)	Total phosphorus (mg/L)	Soluble reactive phosphorus (mg/L)	Dissolved chloride (mg/L)	*E. coli* (C/100mL)
							Storm 1—Continued									
11-19-03	16 35	9.0	92	10.8	7.5	23.6	236.23	4.06	60	[1]0.04	0.23	0.54	0.09	[1]0.06	4.45	E 380
	17 35	8.8	91	10.9	7.4	28.3	242.30	4.14	126	<0.01	0.34	0.55	0.17	0.02	4.32	420
	18 35	8.6	90	11.0	7.5	31.6	244.80	4.17	90	<0.01	0.32	0.57	0.10	0.02	4.25	440
	19 35	8.5	89	11.0	7.4	31.1	243.30	4.15	62	<0.01	0.30	0.57	0.11	0.02	4.20	E 360
	20 35	8.4	89	11.1	7.5	31.8	241.00	4.12	62	<0.01	0.33	0.57	0.09	0.02	4.15	E 360
	21 35	8.2	88	11.1	7.4	31.3	240.30	4.11	64	<0.01	0.35	0.57	0.10	0.02	4.09	E 380
	22 35	8.0	88	11.2	7.4	29.4	238.53	4.09	76	<0.01	0.33	0.58	0.09	0.02	4.16	E 140
	23 35	7.9	88	11.2	7.5	28.1	236.23	4.06	56	<0.01	0.30	0.58	0.10	0.02	4.16	E 190
11-20-03	00 35	7.7	88	11.3	7.5	27.3	233.97	4.03	53	<0.01	0.25	0.60	0.08	0.02	4.24	E 90
	01 35	7.5	88	11.3	7.5	24.1	231.00	4.03	38	<0.01	0.27	0.61	0.08	0.02	4.30	E 110
	02 35	7.4	88	11.4	7.5	26.0	227.70	3.94	47	<0.01	0.27	0.63	0.08	0.02	4.31	E 100
	04 35	7.1	89	11.5	7.5	21.1	220.53	3.85	32	<0.01	0.24	0.64	0.06	0.02	4.39	E 90
	08 35	6.8	89	11.7	7.5	16.7	207.93	3.68	24	<0.01	0.25	0.64	0.06	0.02	4.43	160

[1] Outlier value not used in regressions.